P9-EJJ-521

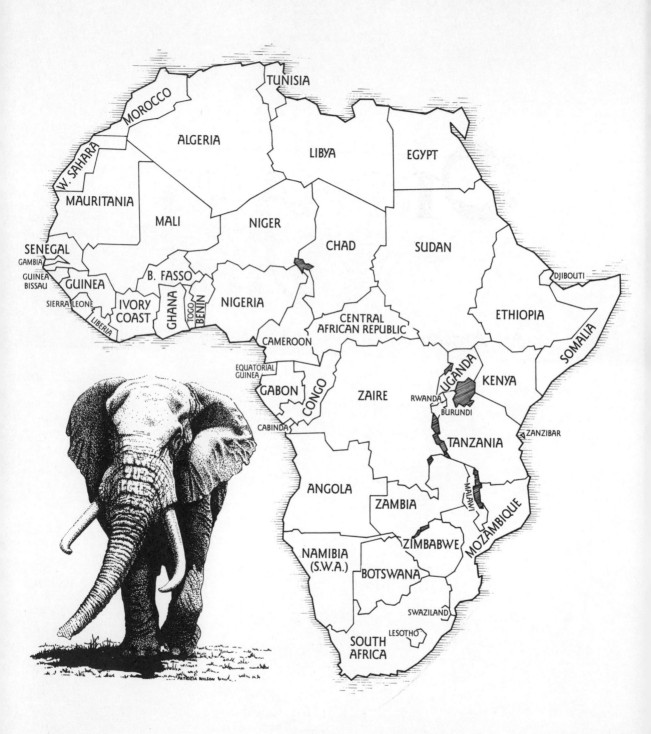

TUNISIA
MOROCCO
W. SAHARA
ALGERIA
LIBYA
EGYPT
MAURITANIA
MALI
NIGER
SENEGAL
GAMBIA
GUINEA BISSAU
GUINEA
SIERRA LEONE
LIBERIA
IVORY COAST
B. FASSO
GHANA
TOGO
BENIN
NIGERIA
CHAD
SUDAN
DJIBOUTI
ETHIOPIA
CENTRAL AFRICAN REPUBLIC
CAMEROON
EQUATORIAL GUINEA
GABON
CONGO
SOMALIA
UGANDA
KENYA
RWANDA
BURUNDI
ZAIRE
ZANZIBAR
CABINDA
TANZANIA
ANGOLA
ZAMBIA
MALAWI
MOZAMBIQUE
NAMIBIA (S.W.A.)
ZIMBABWE
BOTSWANA
SWAZILAND
LESOTHO
SOUTH AFRICA

PATRICIA WILSON

ORPHANS OF THE WILD

An African Naturalist in Pursuit of a Dream

by
Vivian J. Wilson

Line drawings by
Paddy Wilson

Wolfe Publishing Company
6471 Airpark Drive
Prescott, Arizona 86301

First published in 1977 by Books of Rhodesia Publishing Co. (Pvt.) Ltd.
(ISBN: 0-86920-162-X) under the title *Orphans of the Wild — The Story Behind Chipangali*

This edition is revised and updated, with a new subtitle,
for publication in the United States of America

Manufactured in the United States of America
Printed March 1988

ISBN: 0-935632-65-4

1988
Wolfe Publishing Co., Inc.
Prescott, Arizona 86301

To my wife
Paddy
and my sons
Kevin and Barry

CONTENTS

FOREWORD

ORPHANS OF THE WILD is the true story of a young lad's dreams to work toward the conservation of wildlife, and how these dreams came to fruition.

As a schoolboy, Viv Wilson spent most of his holidays and weekends "out in the bush" around Natal in South Africa. He had three distinct objectives — to become a game ranger and explore Africa; to work in a museum where he would learn the more scientific and technical aspects of wildlife; and to visit the Antarctic.

As you read this book, you will appreciate the difficulties he experienced in order to achieve his dreams, how he overcame them and then went on to establish the Chipangali Wildlife Orphanage near Bulawayo in Zimbabwe, which is a unique sanctuary for orphaned and problem wild animals.

He became a game ranger and later a research biologist in several African countries, a curator of mammals, and then director of the Natural History Museum in Bulawayo. He also journeyed to the Antarctic, and became the star of a television series which is based on this book and viewed around the world. Viv is the author of two popular wildlife books, and has produced some 50 scientific papers published in recognized scientific journals in different parts of the world.

Throughout his life, this remarkable man has shown incredible and total dedication to achieve his aims, and has always taken on new challenges with unfailing enthusiasm.

Totally supported by his wildlife and commercial artist wife, Paddy (Patricia), Viv established the wildlife orphanage in 1973, and in later years had the invaluable assistance of his two sons, Kevin and Barry. The original concept of the orphanage became a family interest, and up until 1987 they created, ran and funded the Chipangali Wildlife Orphanage.

As the operation grew to become one of Africa's largest privately owned collections of captive wild animals, the Wilson family suggested the formation of a Wildlife Trust which would eventually assume full responsibility of the orphanage. This was achieved in 1982, and for several years the Trust acted only as a fund-raising agent for the orphanage. However, in 1987, after many detailed discussions, the Wilsons and the Chipangali Wildlife Trust agreed that the Trust would take over the responsibility of the orphanage.

The Wilson family then donated all the animals and enclosures, buildings, office equipment, vehicles, etc., to the Trust. But the story does not end there, for the Wilson family is still fully committed and involved in the daily running of the orphanage.

Because of their tremendous success in breeding several species of rare animals in captivity, Chipangali has been recognized as an important breeding center, and the Duiker Research and Breeding Center (explained in the book) is just one aspect of the overall plan.

Each of the Wilsons has his or her own special talents over and above involvement in the running of Chipangali. Viv is deeply committed to research work and is at present conducting a survey of the duikers of Africa, a mammoth undertaking, and is also involved in other research projects in Zimbabwe and throughout Africa. Paddy is the administrator of Chipangali in addition to producing artwork in the form of maps and line drawings for Viv's various popular books and scientific research projects. She is also an accomplished wildlife artist.

Kevin and Barry follow closely in their father's footsteps. Kevin is responsible for training and returning birds of prey back into the wild, while Barry's interests include butterflies and botany. It is remarkable that not one of the family has had the advantage of a formal university education. Yet they are able to manage the sick and injured animals under their care and attend to nearly all the veterinary problems which arise in such a large collection of animals.

If you have seen the Wilson family in action on television in the series called "Orphans of the Wild" (based on Viv's original book) and then read this book, I'm sure you will agree — here is a truly remarkable family.

Sir Athol Evans, K.B.E., B.A., LI.B.

Chairman, Chipangali Wildlife Trust
P.O. Box 1057
Bulawayo, Zimbabwe

ACKNOWLEDGMENTS

I WOULD NOT have been able to establish Chipangali Wildlife Orphanage and then write this book without the help and encouragement of my wife Paddy, my sons Kevin and Barry, and a great many other people; my profound thanks to them all.

My first thanks go to Paddy for helping with the formation of Chipangali. Without her devotion it would not have seen the light of day. She has also helped rear many of the baby animals, organized most of the gardens, and designed and drew the building plans.

The superb line drawings and maps appearing in this book were painstakingly done by her. She helped wherever possible with my research programs and field work.

My sons, Kevin and Barry, have always been a source of inspiration and without their help with the veterinary work at Chipangali and dealing with the many problems with orphaned, sick or injured wild animals, I could not have achieved what I have.

They also helped rear many of the young carnivores (especially lions and leopards), and the antelope, and on many occasions have suffered from bites and scratches. Both boys have also looked after the many species of birds of prey brought to the orphanage. Not only have they reared babies, but also, whenever possible, "hacked" them back to the wild.

Sir Athol Evans, chairman of the Chipangali Wildlife Trust, has been incredible with his wonderful enthusiasm. He has supported us personally through good and bad times and we could not have asked for a more effective and reliable chairman. We are most grateful to him.

It was partly as a result of the formation of the new Trust that Chipangali was finally saved from closing, and to Mrs. Jean Galloway, Miss Elsa Nielsen, Mrs. Dee Payne,

Baron Merick Dergiman, Dr. John Hulme, Mr. Alan Trentham and Mr. Peter Rollason, all Trustees, I would like to extend my very great thanks.

Finally, to Mrs. Sybil Cole, my typist and secretary, very special thanks for all her hard work, and for typing from my shocking handwriting, and often typing some of my work over and over again.

Vivian J. Wilson

*(**Author's Note:** The word "native" is used extensively throughout this book, and in doing so it is not in any way meant to be derogatory or insulting to a specific group; rather, it is used to indicate the people who are native to the land; i.e., Black Africans.)*

ORPHANS OF THE WILD

CHAPTER ONE

CHIPANGALI

THE BODY OF a tiny kudu calf, clubbed to death an hour before, drooped over the shoulders of the native hunter as he strolled into camp. Its beautiful dark eyes were still wet and clear. Had it not been for the crushed skull, I might have imagined the lovely little creature was alive. The umbilical cord was still red and soft. The baby could not have been more than a day or two old, or perhaps born that day.

"Why did you kill this little animal?" I asked. The hunter replied in *ChiNyanja*, the local language, that he was only doing his job and it was part of the work to kill all animals of certain species in his area. Hoping to impress me, as I was the new Bwana about whom he had been told, he then proudly stated that he had also shot its mother.

I knew the hunter was right, and was in fact doing his job. The Game and Tsetse Department of Northern Rhodesia (now Zambia) employed tribal hunters to shoot those particular animals (irrespective of age and sex) which were infested by trypanosomiasis (the disease carried by tsetse flies). He was stationed at a bushcamp called Titimila in the Chipangali area of the country's Eastern Province.

That was Sunday, 12 December 1954. Msatero Mwale, my assistant, and I had left Fort Jameson (now Chipata) at dawn for Chipangali, about 55 miles away. I had arrived in the Eastern Province only a week before to take over as officer-in-charge of tsetse control operations and was travelling as much as possible to get to know my area, which stretched from Mozambique in the south, to Tanganyika (now Tanzania) in the north. The western boundary was the Luangwa River in Zambia, and to the east was Nyasaland (now Malawi). North to south it was about as far as from San Francisco to Los Angeles.

Two of Central Africa's top tsetse entomologists, Bill Steele and John Gledhill, had explained the basic requirements for my new job. The tsetse fly is peculiar to Africa and exists in more than four million square miles — an area larger than the United States. The tsetse (pronounced "tetzee") spreads trypanosomiasis, or sleeping sickness, when it has bitten an infected beast — game or cattle — and then bites an uninfected animal.

At this time in Zambia, tsetse control operations consisted of three major applications: insecticide, clearing bush which the tsetse favored, and selective game elimination.

In theory, if the animals which the tsetse preferred were eliminated, the flies would die of starvation. So native hunters were posted to widely scattered field camps in the large areas to be cleared, and told to shoot every animal they contacted of the selected species. Kills had to be properly accounted for, and the tail of each animal had to be produced with the spent cartridges used. Each hunter was issued 10 to 20 rounds of ammunition (depending on the size of the area covered). Hunting ability was assessed on how many animals were killed compared with how much ammunition was used. So it was to the hunter's advantage if some animals could be killed without using a rifle. The tail from these animals could be matched to spent cartridges on missed shots, making the hunter "appear" more efficient. I loathed the system, for a hunter would club a wounded animal to death, or leave it to die, rather than use a second round of ammunition. The hunter was allowed to keep the meat of all animals shot.

For more than 10 years, the Chipangali remained one of my favorite areas. The actual control portion was about 130,000 acres in the northeast corner of Chipata district. It was bounded to the southeast by the Rukuzi River down which Dr. David Livingstone travelled on his way from Malawi to the Luangwa River. North of Chipangali lay the beautiful, hilly Lukusuzi Game Reserve and to the east, Malawi and the Kusungu Reserve.

The predominantly "sandveld" soil of Chipangali is covered with a large stand of tall trees known to botanists as *Brachystegia* and locally known as *msasa*. Scattered throughout the slightly undulating country are numerous rocky outcrops, and occasionally, large hills. Its most characteristic feature is its drainage system of *dambos*— a seasonally wet area (drainage lines) covered with moderately tall grass, and sometimes trees.

The dambos had typical African names: Titilila, Dwasengwa, Masiatua, Khalikhali, Katete, among others; and the rocky outcrops and hills such lovely sounding ones as Kanjenjezi and Kongwe. The Chipangali, from which the area got its name, is a small stream that flows throughout the year. In places its banks were covered with thick vegetation which formed the main habitat of bushbuck.

I asked Msatero Mwale, who knew the area very well, what Chipangali meant. Without hesitation he said in ChiNyanja: *Malo anali oyela, nyama ambiri, anthu abwino kwambili.* In other words, a "whitish, open place with lots of game and very friendly people"; that is, "open, friendly country." Msatero indicated that for many generations the tribesmen living west of the Rukuzi River had hunted in the Chipangali area which they always found pleasant, cool and open. Although game was generally not that plentiful, it did move in and out from both the Kusungu and Lukusuzi game reserves.

It had rained heavily the night before we visited Chipangali on 12 December. The bush-track we followed was almost completely overgrown with grass, which the vehicle flattened out behind us. Clouds of wet grass seeds covered the windshield and radiator, and the windshield wipers were sweeping continually. When we reached Titimila, the hunters' camp, the radiator was boiling furiously and steam sprayed out in jets. A delightful campsite under a cluster of green msasa trees was found, and we sorted out our *katundu* (gear).

It was 11:30 A.M. when the hunter walked into camp with the baby kudu, only about an hour after our arrival. I watched as the natives flayed the clean fawn-colored skin from the animal. After cutting the meat into strips, they hung it on a pole-rack over a low fire to smoke. Then the hunters and their wives collected knives and departed into the bush to cut up the other kudu, mother of the baby, left where it had been shot.

I accompanied the party through some delightful green but sparse woodland. Water lay in pools everywhere from the previous night's rain. We came across fresh tracks of four elephant — just deep impressions in the soft ground.

An hour later, as we approached the kudu carcass, a large male leopard suddenly sneaked off in front of us. I noticed how much more brightly colored it was than the leopards in the Umfolozi Game Reserve in Zululand. It had a golden-yellow coat with distinct black rosettes, and even though brightly colored, it still blended perfectly with the surroundings and the rays of sunlight streaking through the canopy of trees. It is unusual to see a leopard in the middle of the day, but since the area was remote, all peaceful and quiet, I suppose there was no reason it should not have been out looking for food.

And he had found it — the hunters' kudu! They were angry that the leopard had eaten part of their food supply, but I was delighted at seeing my first Zambian leopard. He made no effort to elude us, but merely sneaked off, as they so often do, for about 200 yards, stopping from time to time to see if he was being followed. At a safe distance he halted, turned around and faced us, then lay down and waited. Through my binoculars I could clearly see his head and large round ears; occasionally he flicked his tail from side to side.

The Africans set about their work enthusiastically and in less than an hour the whole job was finished. On the ground lay a pile of meat to be carried back to camp, and left behind for the vultures, hyena and I hoped, the leopard, was the skin, skull, intestines and stomach of what was once a magnificent beast.

The meat was shared equally among the carriers (two hunters, two women and Msatero) and we set off for camp. Shortly before leaving I took a knife from a hunter and opened the large stomach of the kudu, to see what was inside. I was amazed at the vast quantity of leaves, fruits and pods that were whole, undigested, and obviously identifiable. In the stomach was a large piece of tissue which puzzled me. I cleaned it off with the knife and carried it back to camp with the intention of examining it later. No sooner had we left the remains of the carcass and walked about 300 yards than the leopard was back on the scene, sorting out pieces of meat for himself.

On the way back to camp I found myself asking dozens of questions. Why didn't the hunters capture the baby kudu instead of killing it? Surely it could have been reared and released somewhere else. Why wasn't the skin and skull of the kudu saved; weren't the museums interested in them? As the female kudu was lactating heavily, I wondered if anyone knew what the chemical composition of the milk was and if it had ever been analyzed. What about the uterus and ovaries of the female? Perhaps some institution working on reproductive physiology of mammals could use them for histological work. How much did wildlife fieldworkers know about the food and feeding habits of kudu and other species; if the stomach contents of that kudu were washed and sieved, surely there would be a lot of plant material that could be identified? Both external and internal parasites were seen on the kudu and I wondered how much was known about the ticks and worms that infested them.

The questions I found myself asking seemed endless and before I knew it, we had covered the four miles back to camp, by which time I was confused and depressed. I made up my mind that day to learn as much as possible from other fieldworkers, and also to make some attempt to save some of the valuable material from the animals shot.

I was very young, only 22, and had very little authority as I had only recently joined the Game Department. Consequently I could not change any of the things I disapproved of. In fact, my experience was so limited that I knew little about what was going on.

4

However, I did decide that if an animal had to be shot, I would learn as much as possible and collect all the available data.

While the tribesmen were cutting the meat into long strips and hanging it on the rack over the fire to dry, I collected a bucket of water from the spring and washed my own chunk of meat. It looked quite different when clean. It had a strange shape, was large and flat, and all over it were lumps of reddish tissue less than an inch in diameter. It suddenly dawned on me that this was the afterbirth of the female kudu, and the red, round lumps were cotyledons of the placenta.

As usually happens, female antelope and carnivores will eat the afterbirth soon after producing their young. Obviously, as the placenta had not already been digested, the female had produced her baby very shortly before being shot — probably that very morning. My desire for knowledge being awakened, I made notes of what had happened, and drew field sketches of the placenta.

At 4:30 P.M., Msatero and I walked to the Kanjenjezi Hills which formed the southern boundary of the Lukusuzi Game Reserve. Titimila camp was situated on the tsetse perimeter-line (merely a line of demarcation for control purposes) and between this and the Lukusuzi Reserve was a corridor about five miles long where no hunting took place. Beyond, Msatero said, were vast numbers of elephant, sable, roan, zebra, hartebeest, rhino and many other species.

Although I had been in the country for little over two months, and in eastern Zambia for a fortnight, I had already learned a good deal of the ChiNyanja language. I loved the African names for the animals and it was these that I memorized first: *Nyalubwe* (leopard), *Ngoma* (kudu), *Njati* (buffalo), *Njovu* (elephant), *Insa* (duiker), *Kasenya* (grysbok), and many others.

A mile north of Titimila we came across a herd of 17 elephant, and in it were several very small babies. I was pleased that they were not in the tsetse area, for had they moved across the perimeter, one or more of them would have been shot.

On being disturbed they screamed, opened their ears wide and ran off toward the Lukusuzi. That afternoon we also saw two herds of zebra and a large female black rhino with a small calf, so young that there were still no signs of its horns. As soon as she scented us, although I doubt if she actually saw us, the rhino ran off into the woodland, with the calf following closely behind. She made sure that she was not going too fast, so as not to leave her offspring at any great distance behind her.

Over the years that followed I got to know this female very well as she had a well-defined territory, and a beautiful pair of nicely proportioned horns. On reaching the

5

top of the hills, we sat for a short time gazing at the beautiful country. We could see in all directions, and the open dambo country of the Lukusuzi which lay north of us looked green and welcoming. To the south the many rocky outcrops in the Chipangali area stuck out like great beacons above the dense forest, broken only by the lines of the dambos. Even further south, the hills near Chipata were clearly visible, and in the far distance the Machinga escarpment, west of the Luangwa Valley, could be seen about 60 miles away.

Back at camp that night, as I sat alone, I experienced a sense of gratitude at being alive and enjoying the wonders of nature. I was content on my own and did not miss human company. The campfire gave me sufficient light to write in my logbook, and I recorded the day's events. Hyenas were yelping in the distance and I wondered if they had found the remains of the kudu carcass. They would certainly leave very little for the other scavengers. As I wrote, I thought of Ian Player in Zululand and was grateful for his training at Ndumu Game Reserve. When we young rangers returned to camp at the end of each day, Ian would make us do our homework like a bunch of schoolboys. He insisted that we write in our diaries and record all we had seen and done. I had found it a nuisance but have come to see the value of it today. He was (and is) a great man with fine ideals and it was a privilege to have worked with him. By the way, Gary Player, of U.S. golf fame, is Ian's brother.

That night I slept peacefully under the tall msasa trees and looking up at the stars, thanked God for such a wonderful world. I made resolutions that I have managed to stick to for more than 20 years; one of them was never to waste an animal. If it had to be killed for some reason, I would obtain as much information as possible from it. Another was to attempt to rear all baby animals that came my way and not to consent to, nor encourage, their destruction.

My first instructions to the hunters next morning concerned baby animals: If an adult female was shot with young at heel they should try to capture it. It should not be destroyed but brought to me for attention. If the baby was too large, then naturally it should be destroyed rather than left to die a lingering death by itself. I felt that if I could rear the babies I would rather release them in an area where they would be safe and where no hunting took place.

In the week that followed, I walked many miles in all directions, spending many hours in the Lukusuzi Game Reserve where I saw countless animals. I had noted that game was sparse around Chipangali. I did come across the occasional elephant, zebra, kudu and other large animals, while the smaller species were generally more plentiful. In the Lukusuzi, however, the picture was completely different — game abounded and was extremely tame.

6

Kongwe Hill in Chipangali area
— Eastern Zambia

Author with African hunter in Chipangali (note game fence)

The day before I was due to return to Chipata, one of the hunters came into camp carrying a baby duiker. He had shot its mother and, as instructed, had captured the baby. "Now what?" I thought, as he presented me with a beautiful little creature with a soft, long coat, large black eyes, erect ears and weighing under two pounds. I was completely nonplused as I took it from him. Had I really done the right thing? (I did not know then that the duiker would one day be a species I would study in depth.)

Again I had to ask myself many questions. How do I feed it? What type of milk? How often do I feed it? Where will I keep it? Perhaps it would have been more humane to have destroyed it rather than attempt to rear it and have all the problems that would follow.

I took another look at its large, black, shiny eyes. It cried, and I was convinced I had done the right thing. Surely it was entitled to live, and I would make it my duty to see that it did. I used a large syringe from my snakebite kit, made a weak mixture of powdered milk, and squirted it down his throat. He was thirsty and drank readily, although at first I virtually had to force him to do so. He already had strong, well-developed, front teeth; he could not have been more than a week or two old. That night I put him in my Land-Rover to sleep but he jumped about for hours and cried continually. Unable to sleep, I moved the vehicle out of earshot. Only then did I doze off. However, I worried most of the night about the little chap, and hoped he wouldn't injure himself in the vehicle.

Next day I returned to Chipata with my orphan and consulted many people on how to feed and rear him. The veterinary department suggested cow's milk diluted with water (50/50). The veterinary officer did say that he had no idea of the composition of duiker milk and that he could be wrong. He also suggested feeding every four hours.

I followed his instructions and next day the little animal had a bad case of diarrhea. Two days later it was dead. I felt ill and depressed over the experience and blamed myself for the death of the little orphan. I consoled myself with the thought that I had tried to save its life, and also was determined to keep trying until I knew what to do.

As I sat looking sadly at the limp little body, I yearned for the proper knowledge and the right facilities to rear and attend to such orphaned animals. It was no more than a dream at the time. Little did I know that my dream would become a reality many years later, at another place called Chipangali — not in Zambia but in Bulawayo, Zimbabwe, hundreds of miles to the south.

But first let me go back to Natal, in South Africa, where it all started . . .

CHAPTER TWO

MY EARLY DAYS

SCORPIO IS MY sign of the Zodiac. I was born on 31 October 1932 in Johannesburg, a city like Butte, Montana, built, literally, on top of underground mines. But though Johannesburg was known as the Golden City, the world in 1932 was in the middle of a terrible economic depression with millions of people out of work.

I was the second in a family of five children. My paternal grandfather had been an engineer in the Liverpool shipbuilding yards and had come to South Africa as a young man. My father, who became a building contractor, was born in the Cape.

But my mother's side of the family went back six generations in South Africa. It was the Fick family, the first arriving in the Cape with other German settlers in 1789. The original Fick's house in Stellenbosch (near Cape Town) was declared a National Monument in 1970 and is now the permanent home of the Rembrandt van Rijn Art Foundation.

General J.C. Smuts, South Africa's prime minister during World War II, was a cousin of my mother, and he was married in the old Fick house in Stellenbosch.

My earliest childhood recollection was of a bitterly cold June day in Johannesburg when I was 10. There was a heavy fall of snow, very unusual for that area. The landscape was transformed and it stirred in me a sudden curiosity about the lands of snow and ice. I remember that it was such joy and fun to go to school that day. Not that I always found school such a pleasure. There are those who say schooldays were the happiest days of their lives. It wasn't like that for me. I skipped school as often as I could; I became allergic to teachers and I grew to hate all forms of academic work.

My love of animals, and of the wild, was developing fast. When I came home from school in Johannesburg one day in January 1942, my mother had a lovely surprise.

9

She had bought a large number of chickens, geese and turkeys. I remember watching them for hours, and loved every one.

My father owned 15 acres of very rocky but beautiful land. Here and in the neighboring hills, I spent many peaceful, carefree hours running barefoot, chasing wild hares and collecting plants and "creepy-crawlies." Jackals, duiker and other small buck abounded in the undeveloped region near our home.

About this time we moved to Natal, South Africa's eastern coast sugar province.

In 1947 my interests in wildlife became more serious. My friend, Ian Dickson, and I spent our school holidays searching for birds' eggs, and within a few years I had a fascinating collection of 600, representing over 100 species. Every spare minute I was out in the bush or on the beach, observing birds and collecting eggs, seashells, crabs or any other of nature's treasures available to a young inquiring mind.

Meanwhile there was still the matter of my formal education. With the move to Durban (Natal) from Johannesburg, I had advanced to a secondary school (Warner Beach) where I was lucky enough to stay until the end of my schooldays.

I was a school prefect (student officer), played rugby football for the school team, and usually won the middle and long distance athletics' prizes. I also played the bass drum in the band. These activities made school more tolerable, but I would much rather have spent all my time doing the "interesting" things.

Little time was devoted to studying, and although I passed my examinations, I was nearly always last in class. The only subjects I enjoyed, and in which I did fairly well, were geography, science and mathematics. It's ironic that I never studied biology, for it was not taught at this school.

December 1949 was a memorable month. I would leave school after matriculating, and as far as I was concerned, would never study again. Little did I appreciate then the importance of a good education, and how much studying I would do later in life. At that time I was interested only in wild animals and the wide-open spaces.

Now out on my own, I had three definite goals: To become a game ranger in some remote national park or game reserve; to work in a museum — but only if I couldn't get a job as a ranger; and to visit the frozen wastes of the Antarctic. (That all three should eventually come true is little short of a miracle!)

I wrote to every game department I could think of, from the Sudan in the north to the Kruger National Park in the south, but oddly enough not to the Natal Parks Board. By far the majority of letters went unanswered, and the few replies I did receive were all the same: "no vacancies" or "too young and inexperienced." I can appreciate today what young people go through when they have the desire for certain work and can't get a foot in any door.

Days became depressing and it was essential to take a job as soon as possible. I had to shelve the idea of working in the bush, but still was determined to fulfill my ambitions. They would have to wait. Besides, my father had other plans for me. Having worked very hard all his life at his trade, he wanted office jobs for his sons. He used to say that we should go to work clean, and return home the same way — with stiff collar and tie. I could think of nothing worse; I hated ties and long trousers!

I was persuaded to answer an advertisement for a job in Durban's main post office, and to my chagrin was accepted. How remote this prospect seemed from my cherished dreams of a life in the African wilds.

Before being imprisoned in the post office, I had one more quick field trip with a couple of friends, cycling to Zululand, a trip of some 125 miles. How wonderful this was. When we arrived at the Tugela River (the boundary between Natal and Zululand), I stood for some time on the bridge, looking down at the muddy water as it raced to the sea. Large fallen trees and other flotsam floated by, and suddenly I spotted the dorsal fin of a large shark. It had obviously swum up from the sea searching for food in the flooded river. I watched it play about in the small waves created by the fast-flowing water and I remember feeling that someday, somehow, I had to be involved with nature.

Before leaving on the cycle trip, my uncle, Lawrence Green, who worked at a fertilizer factory a few miles from home, said he would try to get me a position in the laboratories there. Upon arriving home, to my great delight, I was offered the job. Now two were lined up. My mind was set on the laboratory, my father's on the post office. I won!

Starting as a lab assistant on 1 February 1950, I found the job exciting and rewarding. I was able to move around the large factory collecting samples of acids, fertilizers and other chemicals for analysis. I became friendly with the chief superintendent of the factory who, as a geologist, frequently went into the bush of Natal and Zululand prospecting for phosphates and other minerals. Several times I accompanied him and we were away for days.

I studied after work and took courses in chemistry at the University of Natal and at the Technical College. It looked as if I was set to remain an industrial chemist. In my spare time, however, when I wasn't studying chemistry, I was reading about wildlife. My father gave me a large room in one of our outbuildings which I converted to a museum. In it I housed my collection of birds' eggs, dozens of preserved snakes, mounted game heads, a very large collection of cowrie shells, and many other specimens of nature. I often visited the Durban Museum and was always made welcome by

Mr. Clancey, without doubt the finest ornithologist in Africa.

One of my cherished books at that time (one I have read many times since) was *Edward Wilson of the Antarctic*. It was awarded to me as first prize at Sunday School a few years before. Each reading session increased my desire to visit the Antarctic, although I could see no possibility of doing so.

Many of my weekends were spent camping and collecting snakes. I had many live ones but, lacking proper facilities for large snakes, I kept only small specimens. The large ones were sold to the Snake Park in Durban. From time to time I would capture a large black or green mamba and these were always taken to the park. Payment was about $10 each, and some months I made more selling snakes than I earned at the factory.

In the early 1950's I had a lovely girl friend, Elaine Andreason, a nurse at Addington Hospital in Durban. Her Norwegian father was a lighthouse-keeper on the Natal South Coast, and when Elaine went home on weekends, I would often accompany her. One unfortunate day in May 1951, while staying at her home, I was severely bitten while capturing a large burrowing adder which, in my ignorance, I mistook for a Natal black snake. It struck me on the right index finger, sinking its fangs deep into the flesh. I ripped the monster off with the left hand and it promptly bit me on the left index finger, and then a third time on the side of the hand near my little finger.

Within several minutes my hands began to swell. Very sharp pains were felt at the site of each bite and thin watery blood oozed from each puncture. Within 15 minutes the fingers around the bites turned a bluish color. I bathed my hands in warm water, which helped relieve the pain, but the swelling increased. I was rushed to a doctor who administered antivenin — a total of 30 milliliters, two at the site of each bite and the balance in the triceps, divided equally between the two arms. A steady throbbing pain continued around each wound and the swelling increased.

The doctor sent me to the closest hospital, at Umbogintwini. The pain became more intense, and by the time I arrived at the hospital an hour and a half later, the swelling had reached my elbows. Five hours after being attacked my shoulders were swelling; painful throbs continued where I was bitten. My arms were put on a pillow on my stomach. Dizziness and violent vomiting followed, and I felt a severe burning sensation in my fingers. Calcium gluconate injections were given and pethidine was injected intramuscularly in the shoulder. During the sleepless night, throbbing pain reached the armpits, and both arms took on hideous colors.

Next day the glands in my neck, groin and armpits were swollen and by the second night the fingers had become a dark greenish-yellow. Large blood blisters developed at each bite. These were incised four days after I was admitted to hospital, and allowed

Egyptian cobra, one of the many snakes in Viv Wilson's collection

to drain. Six days after being bitten, gangrene developed around the fang punctures, and the fingernails on both index fingers fell off, as did the flesh, exposing the bones. To aggravate my condition, serum rash appeared and covered my whole body from the soles of my feet to my head.

Treatment continued day after day. After two weeks the swelling decreased at last. The fingers, however, gave a lot of trouble. Even when I was finally discharged from the hospital, a month later, they had not healed. For three months I was prone to "blackouts," and flesh on the fingers sloughed periodically. They remained immovable for several months. Five months later, the right index finger was still very painful and not healing properly, and I thought it might have to be amputated. Fortunately, the doctor decided on a less drastic measure and the lower joint was stiffened instead. The operation was successful and the finger then healed perfectly.

A month later both hands were in good shape — except for the stiff finger, periodical sloughing of the skin, and large dents in both fingers where the gangrene had eaten away the flesh. (Ironically, the right index finger that the doctor had done so much to save was amputated 25 years later after it was badly mauled by one of my lions.)

I now believe that the original injection of antivenin into the site of the bites was a mistake because the fingers were already very swollen and painful, and the local injection only aggravated the condition.

While I was in the hospital, my father decapitated all my snakes at home. I am sure he thought that my painful experience would be the end of my snake-catching. In fact, it had just the opposite effect. I was even more determined to study snakes, and to avoid making the same mistake again.

Toward the end of 1953, the factory chief and I went on another prospecting journey in northern Zululand, searching several days for minerals near Ingwavuma. On this trip I decided to delay no longer my efforts to find work as a ranger. Working at the factory lab nearly four years, the call of the great outdoors had become too strong.

My father was disappointed; he felt I would never get rich working with game and wildlife, whereas there was a future for me as a chemist. He was quite right, and I have never denied it.

I wrote again to the various game departments in Africa. Replies were received from Kenya, Sudan, Uganda, Nyasaland and Southern Rhodesia, all saying that they preferred "local men" who were familiar with the country and could also speak the local African languages. There were no replies from Zululand, the Belgian Congo, Northern Rhodesia, Tanganyika, Bechuanaland or Portuguese East Africa.

14

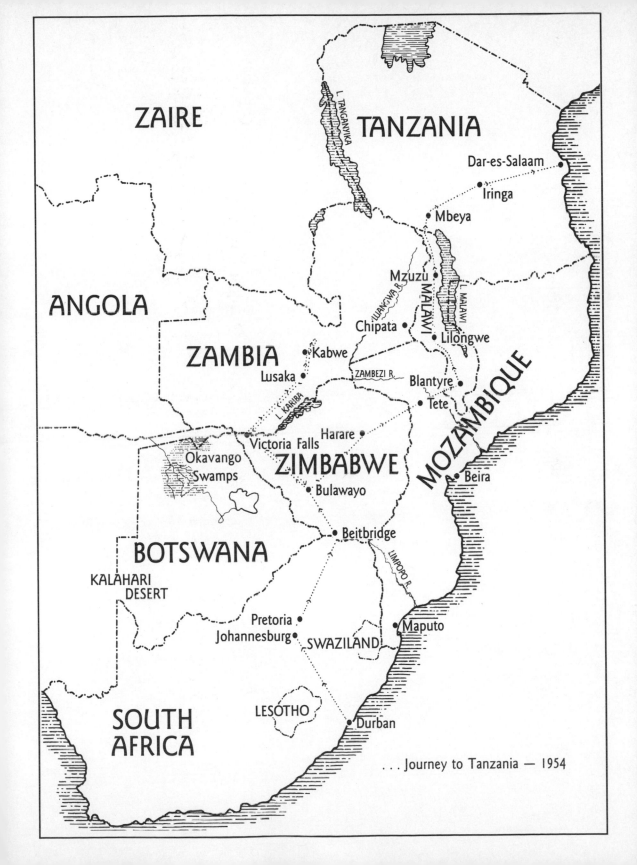

... Journey to Tanzania — 1954

I decided to go north myself, see what the countries looked like, and at the same time try to get a job. I had saved quite a bit of money and I took a month's leave, intending to buy a car and travel by road. However, I decided to keep my cash and hitchhike instead.

I set off in January 1954 with a suitcase, a notebook and many maps of Africa. I was not quite sure of my destination but hoped to reach Tanganyika. With no ties and no commitments, I felt as free and independent as the animals I so much wanted to study and protect.

Luck was present from the start; I was on the road at 5:30 A.M. and completed 400 miles the first day. Within two days I had crossed into Rhodesia, covered over 1,000 miles, and was well on the way to Tanganyika.

The third day was spent in Bulawayo, where the director of the National Museum told me there were no vacancies and pointed out that I was not qualified for such specialized work. He said it would be almost impossible to get a post in the museum. (Thirteen years later I joined the National Museum as mammalogist and within two years became its director.)

I left for Victoria Falls and reached Chilanga near Lusaka two days later. My stars and kind motorists were certainly rushing me north. At Chilanga I called on the director of the Game and Tsetse Department, reminding him of my job application. There still were no openings, he said.

The road to Tanganyika had been washed away by very heavy rains and would be impassable for at least a week. I decided to go back to Bulawayo, then to Salisbury (now Harare) and onward via Tete in Mozambique, through Nyasaland to Tanganyika.

I reached Blantyre in two days, after spending a night on the mighty Zambezi at Tete. It was an exhilarating experience to stand on the banks of that great river and see Africa in such a spectacular setting. Dugout canoes and other small boats moved up and down the river; the whole town was a hive of activity.

I was offered a lift in a truck driven by an African, as far as Lilongwe in central Nyasaland. He was a chatty pleasant fellow and on the long journey, he tried to teach me a few words of ChiNyanja. Depositing me at Lilongwe Hotel, his parting words were *Zikoma bwana*, "Thank you, sir." It was I who needed to thank him — the first of many Nyasalanders to make me feel welcome. That night at the Lilongwe Hotel, little did I realize that I would pass many more nights there in years to come, and that I would work in the game department in Chipata, Zambia, only 100 miles away.

A friendly district officer took me to Mzimba the next day, where I was his guest for the night at the government rest house. His descriptions of the great and beautiful lake, the wildlife, and the people of the Nyika Plateau were enthralling. Years later I travelled extensively in the area, undertook a mammal survey of the Nyika, and wrote a scientific paper on its herptofauna.

The next day I waited hours before the first vehicle came. It was a Land-Rover, and the African driver was going to Rumphi in northern Nyasaland. We traversed miles and miles of broken, hilly country, and saw very few people and not many villages. The vastness and emptiness of Africa was all around us.

We reached Rumphi mid-afternoon and I immediately loved the little settlement. A vast grove of tall palm trees towers over the center of the town and gives the area a truly tropical atmosphere. It was no longer easy to hitchhike in this remote part of Africa; very few vehicles were on the road, trucks or Land-Rovers, and then only going a few miles. I refused lifts that would leave me stranded in the middle of nowhere.

Hardly anyone, white or black, could understand why a young person should be hitchhiking from Natal to distant Tanganyika. Some felt that I would get lost or killed on the way, but at no time while travelling thousands of miles, and with dozens of different people, did I ever experience difficulty or danger.

After a very rough two-day journey, I found myself in Mbeya in Tanganyika. Then came a series of quick lifts to Dar-es-Salaam where I spent two peaceful and relaxing days. I loved every minute in that exotic and fascinating city and could quite easily have stayed there. The harbor is quite beautiful with its tall palm trees providing an ever-moving fringe as they sway in the sea breezes. The water is so clear and blue, you can see fish swimming fathoms below.

Time was running out and there were no job openings. I caught a plane back to Johannesburg, boarded a train for Durban, and arrived home 27 days after leaving — a round trip of nearly 5,800 miles. What an anticlimax! After such a fascinating and exciting journey, and after seeing so many new places and beautiful sights, I had to return to my job at the laboratory. I was truly disappointed that my long trip had not been more fruitful, and that I hadn't found a post as a game ranger.

On my first day back at work, a reporter from the *Natal Mercury* interviewed me and wrote of my long trek north specifically to find a job as a game ranger. Next day there was a phone call from the Natal Parks, Game and Fish Preservation Board, inviting me to contact them about work. This I did and the director was most encouraging. In offering the job, he pointed out that a ranger's work could only be done by a keen and dedicated person.

I began life, at last, as a game ranger on 1 May 1954, and was posted to the Umfolozi Game Reserve. I was one of the happiest men alive. It had taken four-and-a-half years to get what I really wanted; yet I never regretted my time spent in the laboratory.

CHAPTER THREE

UMFOLOZI GAME RANGER

M Y DAD WAS RIGHT, I would never get rich working for a game department, as I soon realized when told that my starting salary would be $40 per month plus a cost-of-living allowance of $16. So my income dropped a great deal when I left the factory lab to work in Zululand, but this did not worry me in the least. I would have worked for nothing, and the fact that I was to be paid for doing something I enjoyed was the fulfillment of my most cherished ambition.

I started at the Umfolozi Game Reserve on 4 May 1954, beginning a wildlife career that was to continue for more than 30 years. It took only a day to settle in at Umfolozi, and the next morning I was out in the bush with an African game guard, observing all that was going on.

Most of the Umfolozi Reserve lies between two beautiful rivers, the Black Umfolozi which the Zulus call *Mfolozi emngama* in the north, and the White Umfolozi *(Mfolozi emhlope)* in the south. The reserve extends from the confluence of these two great rivers west for more than 17 miles to a range of hills. It is very rolling and broken country intersected by a great number of seasonal streams flowing into the two main rivers; most of the streams, however, contain water only during the rainy season. The White Umfolozi has a sandy bed for most of its course, and lower down it opens into vast sandbanks and reedbeds. The river frequently ceases to flow during the dry months, leaving only occasional pools along its length.

The Black Umfolozi, on the other hand, is a well-wooded, perennial river which, during the rains, is capable of becoming a raging torrent covering vast areas. I often felt that the Black Umfolozi River formed an effective natural barrier, preventing the movement of some species of game, especially zebra and wildebeest, to and from the game reserve, for it had numerous rough rapids and large, deep pools for several miles.

Along the main river, several species of wild fig trees could be seen and in places these often formed a long, wide line on the banks. Some of the trees grew to a tremendous size, while away from the main rivers the vegetation was generally acacia veld, of which many species occurred. I loved the great candelabra tree with its white sap. This tree, together with the paper-bark tree, was common away from the rivers and on the hills. The latter trees form the bulk of the browse for game.

The Umfolozi Game Reserve and surrounding country had been occupied by the Zulus and other clans for decades before it was evacuated in about 1882, and I understand it was left unpopulated until 1897 when it was finally proclaimed a game reserve.

I kept a detailed diary of everything that happened at Umfolozi and noted every animal seen. This may seem to be a tall order but it wasn't really so, as hunting by tsetse-control hunters had ceased only a few years previously and very little game had survived. There were several large storerooms at Mzimba (the camp where I lived at Umfolozi) and these were full of skins of the various animals destroyed. I will always remember the hundreds of duiker, bushbuck and nyala skins, and the skins of many other species.

To give some idea of the game in the Umfolozi Reserve and the corridor between the Umfolozi and Hluhluwe reserves, I quote from my diary:

6 May 1954
Saw 13 white rhino, 8 wildebeest, 4 zebra, 2 steenbok and 1 duiker over a distance of 19 km on foot. The wildebeest and zebra were seen in the corridor between the Umfolozi and Hluhluwe game reserves as none existed in the Umfolozi proper.

29 May 1954
Saw 7 kudu, 19 zebra, 3 duiker, 1 steenbok, 1 reedbuck and 6 white rhino over a distance of 24 km on foot. All seen in corridor. This is the greatest number of animals I have seen in a single day since arriving at Umfolozi, where I have been now for almost a month.

21 June 1954
Patrolled the corridor between the Umfolozi and Hluhluwe game reserves where game was certainly more plentiful than in the Umfolozi. The following animals were seen over a distance of 26 km: 22 warthog, 7 waterbuck, 1 duiker, 8 reedbuck, 1 bushbuck, 4 square-lipped rhino, 1 black rhino and 11 zebra.

The square-lipped (white) rhino was one of the most common large mammals in the area in early 1954, because it was the only species spared during the game-elimination operation. The slaughter had started in 1942 and had stopped 10 years later. It was estimated that at least 550 white rhino existed there in early 1954. At least 70,000 animals died as a result of the tsetse campaign, of which 12,834 were warthog, 22,232 bushbuck and 20,461 duiker.

Common grey duiker, one of the species shot in large numbers during the tsetse fly campaign in the Umfolozi Game Reserve

White rhino in the Umfolozi Game Reserve, Zululand, South Africa

In spite of the vast numbers of animals killed before I arrived, there was still quite a number of waterbuck and kudu about, and warthog were seen on almost every trip into the bush. Duiker, bushbuck and bush pig were plentiful and appeared to have thrived in spite of the shooting. Very few buffalo were present and I believe that those seen in the corridor had broken out of the Hluhluwe Reserve. Wildebeest and zebra were also scarce; only occasionally were any seen in the corridor, and none in the Umfolozi proper — between the Black and the White Umfolozi rivers. Although reedbuck, steenbok, nyala, impala and klipspringer were not plentiful, we did see them occasionally.

As for predators, leopards were plentiful and often found near the White Umfolozi. Although the shy hyenas were seldom observed, we often heard them at night. On many occasions while camping on the dry sand of the White Umfolozi, hyenas would come close to our camp and their piercing yells filled the night air in a frightening and eerie way.

In one month, three dead pythons were found in the dry Umfolozi riverbed within about a half mile of each other, apparently killed by a leopard. Leopard tracks and many teeth marks on the large reptiles clearly indicated their responsibility for the killing. Perhaps a particular leopard had a distinct dislike for the serpents and killed them merely for the sake of doing so. None of the pythons was eaten or even nibbled at, but simply left where they had been killed.

The largest of the snakes, a female, measured 19 feet and must have weighed 175 pounds. I skinned her but unfortunately the skin was so full of teeth-holes that it was not worth keeping. The other two pythons were males, one over 14 feet and the other only 11 feet. Pythons were very plentiful in the Umfolozi Reserve, and I often saw them sunning themselves on fallen trees on the banks of the two rivers.

Early one morning in July 1954, Mr. Foster, who was in charge of the reserve, and I were driving along a rough road over mPila Hill when we noticed a dead hare — killed by a vehicle the night before, and a large sand snake. We watched as the snake made repeated attempts to swallow the hare. At first it swallowed a hind leg, reached the body and gave up. It then tried another leg, with the same result. The snake eventually found the front of the hare and, opening its mouth as wide as it could, latched onto the nose. It tried desperately to swallow the hare, but finally realized that it was impossible, and slithered off into the dry grass.

In late July, two game scouts and I were sitting quietly at the junction of the two rivers watching the head, or rather the snout and eyes, of a large crocodile. We had been there for about an hour and a half and in that time it had not moved. The same amount of its nose and eyes protruded above the water and it lay motionless, as if dead. The river glided along noiselessly in the shade, against the swelling reeds and sedges which formed a flexible palisade up its moist sides. To the north of the reeds was a cluster of trees, the leaves of which were still soft and moist, not yet stiffened and darkened under the intense heat.

From a recess in this mound of foliage, a bushbuck female emerged and walked about, unconcerned, as it fed on fallen acacia leaves, occasionally lifting its head to nibble on fresh leaves. The crocodile saw the bushbuck at the same time we did, and without a sound or the slightest visible movement it disappeared. There was not as much as an air bubble to indicate that it had submerged. We waited quietly as the magnificent bushbuck, with its beautiful red coat and bright white spots, fed closer and closer to the water's edge. Then she nonchalantly entered the water to a depth of 9 or 10 inches and began to drink. There was still no sign of the crocodile. After quenching its thirst the doe turned about slowly and started walking out of the water, much to my relief.

Suddenly, without warning, the crocodile lunged from the water and caught the bushbuck by one of its hind legs. It made no effort to drag its prey into the water immediately but held on tightly as the poor antelope screamed and struggled. The three of us stood up and yelled, hoping to frighten the crocodile, but it ignored us. How I wished we could have helped. Unfortunately we were on the other bank of the river and some distance away. When we did manage to disturb the croc, it merely reversed into the water, pulling and dragging the petrified doe along with it. Once in deep water it submerged completely, and the cries of the doe were stilled as she, too, disappeared into the murky depths. A series of air bubbles rose to the surface, and a few minutes later all was peaceful and quiet again. How very sad, and yet how natural the whole scene was. I left the area feeling very empty, and yet I knew that this was how nature ordained it.

The day came when I had to shoot my first white rhino. A game scout named Mkageni was patrolling in the White Umfolozi River area when he discovered a dead white rhino calf which had been gored in the stomach. He also heard the tremendous noise of two animals fighting, and went to the scene. He found that one was badly gored, and reported the entire episode to Mr. Foster at Mzimba.

I was sent to investigate, and told to destroy the wounded animal if necessary. Mkageni and I left immediately, and within 30 minutes were at the carcass of the baby rhino. It was very small and could not have been more than a couple of weeks old. We ran to the area where the two rhino bulls were fighting; the banging of horns and the snorting could be heard hundreds of yards away. They had knocked down dozens of small trees in their frantic attempts to gore each other.

We crept up as close as possible, and the rhino, although they could obviously smell us, took no notice. Blood was streaming from the base of the anterior horn of the larger bull and only a few minutes later the horn was knocked off. It left a large, open, bleeding wound. Upon losing his horn he could no longer fight and made no further attempt to protect himself; he went crashing off into the bush with the smaller bull following closely behind, snorting loudly. During the 10 minutes or so that I watched the great beasts fight, I saw no large body wounds on either, although both had small bleeding gashes. As they disappeared into the thickets I told Mkageni that apart from the one which had lost his horn, they appeared to be in reasonably good shape and I thought both would survive.

Mkageni said he thought it was another rhino that was injured, so we started a search. An hour later we found the badly wounded animal, a large female. She had wandered to the White Umfolozi to drink and was standing on the bank looking down at the water, so weak she could hardly move. She had left a large trail of blood from a huge open wound in the chest. The kindest thing was to put her down, and a single shot from the .303 rifle into the brain quickly ended her suffering.

Close examination showed that she had two broken ribs and pierced lungs, and would not have lasted much longer. She was also lactating very heavily, obviously the mother of the dead calf. We removed her horns, took photographs of the wounds and left the carcass for the many hyena in the area. Back at the dead calf, I removed the head, for I wished to keep the skull to study the teeth of so young a rhino.

It appeared that when the bulls were fighting, the calf was accidentally killed and the mother gored. Mkageni, who had worked for many years with white rhino, said this had happened before. Mr. Foster confirmed that he had also witnessed that sort of thing.

When I left Umfolozi several weeks later for Ndumu Game Reserve, Mr. Foster gave me the horn of the female I had shot; also the skull of the baby. Although I was pleased to have the specimens, I regretted that they had to die under such unfortunate circumstances.

That night, back at my camp, I sat outside looking up at the heavens. The sky was clear, startlingly clear, and the twinkling of the stars seemed to be but throbs of one body, timed by a common pulse. Over the horizon rose the wasting moon, now dull and greenish-yellow, like tarnished brass. It did not seem to be the customary hue as its light shone on the logs of my cabin. It appeared that God was palpably present in the country in which I now lived, and that the devil had been left behind in the towns. I did so much love the Umfolozi Game Reserve, for it gave me my first

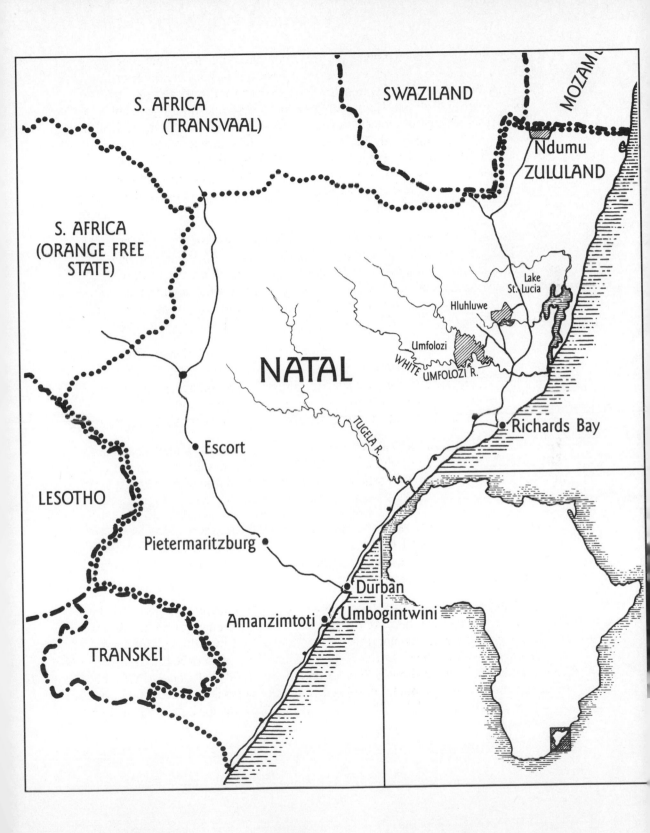

taste of life in African wilds. The first of my three ambitions had been realized. I was indeed a game ranger, working in the wild amongst the creatures I loved so much.

Everything was so new. I realized how little I knew about wildlife, of bushcraft, in fact anything to do with the bush. I was avidly keen to learn, and fortunate that my first teacher was Mr. Foster, who was then about 60 years old and had an excellent knowldege of everything around him.

When I first arrived at Umfolozi I was extremely cautious of the great white and black rhino. As a youngster I had read how dangerous the black rhino can be, and over the three decades that followed, I had many experiences with that temperamental beast, not only in the Umfolozi but also in Zambia and then in Rhodesia. I still treat it with great respect.

Although I had seen a number of black rhino in the reserve during my stay, I had not been close enough to examine them properly. They were not nearly as common as the white rhino and it is doubtful there were as many as 10 in the whole Umfolozi. The main population was in Hluhluwe.

My first nasty experience occurred on 9 May 1954. Two game guards and I were patrolling the corridor when we suddenly noticed a rhino rolling in the mud in a small pan. He was a young animal, perhaps three-quarters grown, and completely covered in mud. The pan in which he was wallowing was nearly dry, for the surface water had been trampled into mud by the game. It was an open area with only a few small bushes about and an occasional large acacia tree. I wanted a good photograph of a black rhino so I crept up and at about 30 feet away, took a couple of shots. The wind was in my favor and he could not smell me; the mud had completely covered his eyes, so he could not see me. As I moved another step closer he must have heard me, for he stood up immediately, spun around and faced in my direction. He was very suspicious, holding his head low to the ground and moving it from side to side, all the while opening and closing his nostrils.

Suddenly the mud covering his eyes fell off and he saw me instantly. Without hesitation he charged; I flew with unbelievable speed up a small acacia tree and into its branches. The tree trunk was about eight inches in diameter but as I lifted my legs off the ground, he struck the tree with his shoulder as he passed. I was knocked down from where I clung, and a large thorn penetrated deep into the side of my wrist and broke off. Bleeding profusely and much shocked, I regained my senses and was helped back to camp, a very subdued young ranger. But my suffering was not yet over.

Mr. Foster did not spare his words, bursting out with some of the worst language I had heard in many a day! He clearly said that he had no sympathy for me, and that I had committed a foolhardy act. When I sheepishly told him I still had the thorn embedded in my arm, he was even more annoyed, for it now meant he would have to take me to the hospital at Mtubatuba to have it removed. The journey was strained and not much conversation passed between us. My arm was very painful and throbbed greatly. The process of removing the inch-long thorn was no easy matter, and from the pain that I suffered, I felt that the doctor sympathized more with Mr. Foster than with me. As a result of that little mishap I learned to respect the black rhino; and yet, in spite of that, I was to experience four more accidents with them over the years.

The white rhino is another kind of animal altogether. During my work in Umfolozi I learned much about the species and on many occasions I would walk right up to them. In fact, the other young game ranger and I used to compete to see who could slap the most rhino on the backside. We would creep up to one and then belt it with a stick on the behind. As the rhino spun around, we would run off into the bush. It was good thing Mr. Foster did not know of that, for I am sure he would have had us dismissed. Looking back on it, it was foolish to take such chances, but then, as young men, I suppose we were trying to prove that we were daring and brave.

Once a week it was necessary to go to the Hluhluwe Reserve to shoot wildebeest for camp meat. Hluhluwe had an abundance of game, especially wildebeest. Each week I would shoot two, and I confess that I hated the job. However, it was one of my duties, and the task was done as cleanly as possible.

During the dry season, when the White Umfolozi no longer flowed, pools still remained throughout the stretch of the river in the Umfolozi. It was at these pools that rhino and other animals got their water, and from time to time rhino would get stuck in the sand or mud; if not helped out, they would eventually die. One evening a couple of African game guards and I found a young female rhino stuck in some soft sand. She had obviously tried to get to the pool and after walking part-way across the dry riverbed, had sunk in to her knees. As we approached she began to struggle and the more she moved, the deeper she sank. We watched her for 20 minutes or so, not knowing what to do; then the game guard mentioned that twice before he had helped Mr. Foster get rhino out of similar situations.

The game guards carried small axes, and they cut a couple of long, stout poles which we rammed under her belly. After much heaving and sweating we were able to turn her over. An hour later she was standing completely exhausted on the hard bank of the river so tired that we could touch her. In fact, we actually pushed her along the last section of sand and up the gently sloping river bank. During the whole operation she made no attempt to charge, or even raise her head. The next day we went back to the river and she was still in the area, but had joined up with another female and a young bull.

Most of our work in the Umfolozi was done on foot. There was only one vehicle at the station and that was for the use of Mr. Foster. The only time we rode in it was when he took us to some distant part of the reserve, where he would drop us off and we would walk back to camp. He felt that this was good for us. We were never mollycoddled. Often we were taken 20 or 25 miles away and "forced" to trek back. He didn't put it as bluntly as that. Instead, he would suggest that we patrol the reserve on the way home.

The other young game ranger and I had a song we'd sing about Mr. Foster — mainly when we were walking home. It went something like this:

Up in the morning, out in the day,
walk like a devil for our pay,
while lucky old Foster has nothing to do,
but ride in his truck all day . . .

As time passed, we grew to love the long, hard walks, and we certainly got to know the reserve. And we saw much more than we would have from a vehicle. In spite of the hard time Mr. Foster gave us, we liked and respected the old man.

After three short months at Umfolozi I was moved north to Ndumu Game Reserve to join Ian Player. We were to help survey the reserve and to cut boundary lines. Although I loved the Umfolozi Reserve, I was delighted to have the opportunity to go north to the Portuguese East Africa (now Mozambique) border, the possibility of working with different game animals being the chief lure.

CHAPTER FOUR

NDUMU

NDUMU GAME RESERVE lies in the northeastern part of Zululand with the Great Usutu River as the northern boundary. Across the river is Mozambique. The reserve covers 25,000 acres — a lush, mostly low-lying, well-watered area. The tropical vegetation, large pans, vast marshes and the two beautiful rivers, the Pongolo and Usutu, make it one of the loveliest and most peaceful areas in Africa.

BagaBaga, Banzi, Polve and Lake Nyamiti, the very names of the pans have a magic which conjure up visions, and the Great Usutu River was to me the best of all. We travelled extensively by boat as it was the only way to see the banks of luxuriant vegetation along both rivers. How exciting to move through the vast mud flats, and to visit the fantastic island called Nagri.

Ian Player was a dynamic person, a great clown; he kept me in fits of laughter with his antics and facial expressions. He could also be very serious, and I learned to respect his moods, likes and dislikes.

Lake Nyamiti was without doubt my favorite spot in Ndumu, and extracts from my diary notes of 15 August 1954, show why:

Sacred ibis, glossy ibis and African jacana were seen today. I counted birds with the aid of my binoculars. A flock of 30+ red-billed teal flew in and landed on the shallow water close to a yellow-billed duck. The arrival of the teal set the whole bird community chattering and the cacophony made by hundreds of white-faced ducks was quite deafening.

Close to the birds, in fact surrounded by birds, were eight large crocodiles, two of which were lying with their mouths wide open. About 50 yards away lay 15 hippo, all asleep in the mud, some of them partly submerged in water. Eight white egrets were walking about on the hippo which seemed unconcerned by the constant pecking on their skins. I wonder if they actually felt the egrets walking on them.

On the southern shore of the lake there is a deposit of fossils and shells belonging to the Cretaceous period which occurred at least 80 million years ago. Some of the main fossils found are ammonites and they are plentiful. Several round boulders which had cracked open revealed the presence of perfectly preserved ammonite.

Only a single large bull hippo was on the south shore of the lake.

On the northern shore I watched another herd of hippo, 16 adults and 3 young, and at one spot 26 crocodiles together, basking in the hot sun. As I approached them, all but one large one disappeared into the water. He refused to move and I could have touched him had I wanted to, but I was very cautious. I picked up a stone and hurled it at him, hitting him squarely on the back. Only then did he reluctantly take to the deeper water. I am sure he wasn't sick, just very old, fat and lazy, and unconcerned about humans.

As I walked along the sandy bank I nearly died of fright when a large water leguan shot out of the reeds and passed within inches of me before it dived into the water. For one moment I thought it was a crocodile.

Fish eagles were plentiful and called throughout the morning, and a single bird was watched attacking a goliath heron. The heron was standing in eight or nine inches of water and the eagle continually dived at it. The only responses from the heron were loud croaking noises; it otherwise appeared quite unconcerned. The eagle did not appear to be aggressive, and actually seemed to be enjoying a game.

What a wonderful setting this lake has.

Ndumu in those days was not open to the public and there were no rest houses or other facilities. Apart from a small prefabricated house in which we lived, there was nothing else.

One of my main tasks was to cut the boundary lines of the game reserve. This was done by compass-bearing. Ian and I marked the boundary and later a gang of natives with axes cut the line through the thick bush. This took many weeks and was a pleasant task, for the lines passed through some lovely country and gave me an opportunity to study the birds.

I loved the dense Selene Forest on the south bank of the Usutu, a place alive with birds and monkeys. Once I saw two large troops of samango monkeys, many sunbirds, including the scarlet-throated manico and white-bellied sunbirds, and the beautiful narina trogon. Mangrove and malachite kingfishers were plentiful in the forest close to the river.

Tree orchids grew all over in the forest; almost every large tree supported its own cluster. In one large fig tree with a circumference of 30 feet I found three different orchid species. A large swarm of bees had made a home under the roots of this tree;

Fish eagles at Ndumu Game
Reserve

Hippo in Ndumu Game Reserve, Zululand, South Africa

when they suddenly made an objection to my presence, I beat a hasty retreat. The tree must have been 140 feet high and hundreds of years old.

The banks of the Usutu River were always covered with crocodiles, and pythons were abundant. What perfect habitat for these reptiles. The whole area was untouched by man and apart from a rough bush-track for the Land-Rover, the forest was still primeval, quiet and peaceful — unspoiled and as God had made it.

One misty morning we watched a python about 13 feet long, with a tremendous girth, as he tried to engorge an adult, female nyala. The snake had already swallowed the head and neck of the antelope when we arrived. The jaws of the reptile spread wide over the shoulders of the buck. Alpheus, the senior game guard, and I stood motionless 15 feet away as the snake continued to feed. It obviously could not see us, unconcerned as it was by our presence. Suddenly a change of wind took our scent toward the snake. The effect was immediate. Without hesitation it regurgitated the meal, and within seconds was on its way to the edge of the river. The nyala carcass was still warm.

Pythons were also found on the banks of the Pongolo River. We would see them coiled up on hanging foliage or in branches of fig trees on the river's bank. In early September 1954, a game guard told us he had spotted a very large snake coiled around an overhanging branch and that it had a massive bulge in it. When we arrived at the site two hours later, the snake was still there, basking in the bright sun. It was completely out in the open, no shade whatsoever, and the bulge was indeed enormous. The snake was 15 feet long, and judging by the size of the bulge, it had surely swallowed an animal the size of a female nyala. It made no effort to move, and we did not disturb it lest it disgorge its meal. We figured it was lying in the hot sun to increase its body temperature which would no doubt speed up digestion.

Zululand is known for its great pythons and they are plentiful throughout. Even where cultivation has destroyed the natural habitat, they are still found and, unfortunately, many are accidentally killed in sugar cane fields.

Like the pythons, the crocodiles are equally at home in the Usutu and Pongolo rivers and all the pans, lakes and swamplands of Ndumu. Fish, bird and mammal prey abound in and near the waters for the benefit of these great monsters, and so the crocodile is lord of the swamps.

Lake Nyamiti is one of the finest places in Africa to research crocodile behavior. The lake supports hundreds of them and its relatively small size enables the crocs to be easily counted and studied.

Python, a species very common in the Ndumu Reserve

One bright morning I noticed a small crocodile swimming along with a darter in its mouth. He made no effort to swallow his prey and played about with the dead bird for more than half an hour. From time to time he would drop it in the water, and after grabbing it again, would throw it in the air. At no time did the reptile make an attempt to eat it. Finally it was left floating on the water as the croc simply submerged and disappeared. A few minutes later another crocodile suddenly snapped at the bird, and just that quickly it was swallowed. I suppose one was hungry, and one was not.

The hide of a large hippopotamus is exceptionally thick and tough. I once measured a piece and found it to be more than ¾ of an inch. No wonder crocodiles cannot penetrate hippo skin until it is almost rotten. This was well borne out in the instance of a bull hippo that we found dead in Lake Nyamiti. It was first seen floating near Dhlozo Point and surrounded by about 18 crocodiles. The next day the carcass had been moved, no doubt by the crocodiles, some 100 yards away; there was still no sign it had been touched. It was only on the morning of the fourth day that the crocs managed to open the body. They were tearing pieces of rotten flesh from it. We watched one crocodile get a tight grip on a chunk of meat, then spin over several times to tear the flesh loose. At one time there must have been 80 or 90 of them at the carcass, the water literally wall-to-wall with them. As the feast continued, the carcass was opened up more and more, while the water was swirling with pieces of meat and blood. The whole macabre scene was one of utter horror. That evening, nothing remained of the huge hippo and, strangely, even the water had cleared and settled. Once again the crocodiles had dispersed over the lake, returning to their own favorite resting places.

———————

The samango monkey is referred to as the blue monkey, and several troops lived in the forests along the Usutu and Pongolo rivers. They had become quite tame as a result of our constant visits and we were able to approach quite close to them. Their main diet was leaves and fruits of various trees in the forest, and they also ate flowers when available. Many times I've observed these animals feeding on the flowers of the quinine tree. Like other primates, they are very wasteful eaters. To satisfy their appetite, many more leaves and flowers are removed than are eaten. Often a single bite is taken and the rest of the plant drops to the ground, to be eaten by other animals.

The common vervet monkey was far more numerous in Ndumu than the samango and they tended to occur in the more open country and acacia veld rather than in the dense fig forests on the river banks. However, some could be found in the forests, but not alongside the samango monkey.

Close to our camp at Ndumu lived a pair of Anderson bat-hawks. Each evening as the sun set over the Lebombo Mountains these beautiful, swift hawks would emerge to find food. I did not see them during the day, although I often looked for them. The birds come out at dusk, at the same time the bats commence flying. We watched these birds attempting to catch bats, and on one occasion a bat was knocked out of the sky, falling near us with a thud. I wrote in my logbook that it was probably the yellow housebat, as a number of them were seen near our building at night.

The bat-hawk is normally a rare bird; with its long wings and slender body it is able to travel at great speed. Its prey, be they swifts, swallows, bats or other birds, are caught with its claws, and swallowed whole while in flight. You'll hear them emit a high-pitched noise at dusk, and this continues from time to time while they're hunting.

The giant fruit bat was often seen at night, flying near pans and rivers. During the day they could be found hanging in the old fig trees near the Usutu River. They are the largest of the fruit bats and have a wingspan of more than 20 inches. The little banana bat is at the other end of the size-scale — a very small, lovely creature and plentiful wherever banana trees grow. They will hide in the dry leaves of banana trees, emerging at night to feed.

Another nocturnal mammal at Ndumu, which has a loud piercing cry, is the large bush baby — often heard but seldom seen. The only way to see them is to use a bright spotlight; then their large eyes can be picked up with ease. During the breeding season they call loudly and continuously, chattering away for hours. We once camped on Nagri Island for a few days, and there were at least four bush babies sharing the island with us; they could be heard all night from different points. The main vegetation on the island was acacia trees and in places the bush was very thick, providing plenty of hiding places.

There was also a young honey badger living on Nagri Island. We saw him twice during the day and he appeared unconcerned by our presence. When we approached he would trot off slowly, and made no effort to dive into the long grass or dense bush.

We also found several groups of dwarf mongoose. They remained close to the hollow trees and termite mounds in which they lived, and when disturbed would dive back into their burrows for safety.

Cane rats were plentiful and active in broad daylight, feeding on grasses and other vegetable matter; they were relentlessly poached by the natives living in the reserve.

There were no rhino in Ndumu in 1954; both the black and white rhino were introduced after I left.

I had been at Ndumu for only a month, and was sitting at Lake Nyamiti watching crocodiles one day, when Ian Player handed me a telegram from Northern Rhodesia. It was from the Department of Game and Tsetse Control, offering me a position in the Game Department. It indicated that I would be posted to the Luangwa Valley area in the Eastern Province. I had applied to the Game Department when I passed through Northern Rhodesia in February of that year but had not heard from them since. Now, after almost eight months, came their reply. I loved Ndumu. I had settled in and had in mind several projects to work on. Now I had to make a quick and important decision: whether to go north to the big game country of the Luangwa Valley or stay at Ndumu?

That night back at camp, Ian Player and I spoke about it for hours. We finally agreed that I would be a fool not to take the opportunity of going to the wilds of the Luangwa where many large species of animals occurred in great abundance. The decision was made!

It was a sad day when I left Ndumu by truck for Mkuzi on 29 September 1954. Ian Player wrote this to me:

> When you are far away you can cast your mind back to Ndumu and remember the gleaming waters of Bagabaga with the spurwing geese and the white-faced duck wheeling around, the plaintive shrieks of the fish eagles, the wild calls of the plovers, the whistles of the parrots and the drumming of the woodpeckers; the sight of the giant marula trees silhouetted against a blood-red sunset in the Lebombo Mountains and the euphorbia trees with their long succulent green stems standing like watchful sentries on the skyline; the fading colors of the evening and the grunting of hippos and the last songs of the robin that break the stillness before the croaking of the frogs — and then darkness; the thumping of the native drums and the reflection of the moon's rays on Lake Polwe. Then the first fingers of another dawn steal across the sky to light up the islands of trees towering above the white mists in the valleys, and the beautiful calls of a coucal come from the depths of the tangled undergrowth in the morning . . .

As I read the letter, my eyes filled with tears; it was distressing to say good-bye.

CHAPTER FIVE

ELEPHANTS & URANIUM

I WAS TWENTY-TWO years old when I arrived in central Africa for my new job and quickly realized that I had made the right decision. I was to spend 10 of the finest years of my life in the wide open spaces of the best game country in Africa — Zambia's Luangwa Valley.

My new home was in Chipata, a picturesque valley village. There was no hotel, one bank, several stores, a police station and a club (the Victoria Memorial Institute).

I moved into a small rough house on the outskirts of town and arranged my few possessions. Government furniture was provided so I had no worry about such (to me) mundane matters. Two days later I packed my vehicle and set off with a native game guard for Msoro in the Luangwa Valley. I spent a week there checking staff camps, counting game and generally becoming acquainted with the area.

The seasonal rains had not yet started in earnest and the Lupande was still only a dry riverbed covered with deep, clean sand. There is an ancient joke about "seasonal" African rivers: If you fall into one, stand up and dust the sand off. The locals were getting their water from holes dug deep into the sand, and these same holes were also frequented at night by elephant, rhino and other game. The natives would become most annoyed in the mornings to find the sides of the holes trampled flat, for it meant that to get water for themselves, they had to dig fresh holes or open the old ones.

Rain had fallen about 30 miles away, but none at Msoro. One afternoon my game guard came running into camp to tell me that the river was "coming down in flood." I raced to the river's bank, which by this time had become crowded with locals. There, some 200 yards away, was a sheet of water, about six inches deep, rapidly covering the dry riverbed, a fascinating sight.

Within a minute or so, the water passed us, replacing the river of sand with one of water. It was soon a foot deep. As the wall moved downstream, it washed all the rubbish along with it — sticks and bushes, elephant droppings, indeed everything that had accumulated in the riverbed during the dry season.

The river gradually filled, until it was several feet deep and flooded its banks. It remained full for many months before drying up again during the following dry season. So the whole pattern would continue, as it had done for thousands of years.

———

In addition to being officer-in-charge of tsetse operations in the province, I also had the duties of game ranger in the Chipata region. Soon after my arrival, a herd of elephant raided the maize fields of a tribesman in a nearby village, and I was ordered to destroy one of the great beasts. The policy of the Game Department was to follow the herd, shoot one of the raiders, and give the meat as compensation to the persons whose gardens had been destroyed. The tusks became government property. The theory was that the elephants would be frightened away from villages and gardens.

Apart from my shooting in Zululand of two white rhino, a few zebra and a number of wildebeest, I was inexperienced as a hunter. Now I had to tackle a monstrous thing like an elephant. Armed with a .375 H&H Magnum rifle and 10 rounds of solid ammunition, and accompanied by Msatero Mwale, my gun-bearer, I set out for Mpomwa.

At the village I explained to Yokania, the headman, that I had come to follow the elephants that raided his garden, and that one would be shot. Delighted, he eagerly took me to the mangled garden. I stared in amazement. It looked as if a bulldozer had gone through the maize field; there were acres of flattened plants. I could not have imagined such havoc, and now knew why the government had adopted the policy of giving meat to the villagers as compensation. Yokania said this particular herd had a habit of destroying his crops.

We wasted no time. Yokania rounded up two trackers and we were off after the brutes.

After several weeks of rain, the ground was soft and the long grass had been trampled flat as the herd of about 10 elephants moved through the bush. We walked in single file, two trackers in front, then myself, Msatero behind me carrying my .375, and Yokania taking up the rear.

We trekked slowly through the wet grass, up and down small hills and across many streams. An hour later we were still on the trail. At one place we could see where the herd had stopped to drink from a depression filled with rainwater; they had trampled the area flat. Another hour passed before we came across some very fresh elephant

Elephant bull in eastern Zambia

droppings. One of the trackers placed the back of his hand on them to test for warmness; he excitedly indicated that the animals were not far ahead.

I was suddenly petrified by the idea of having to shoot one of the huge beasts. What would happen if I missed the brain and it charged? Even if I did kill the elephant, what would the remainder of the herd do? Would they charge? I felt a constricting pain in my chest. I told myself it was only nervousness, and that if I was going to do my job well, I would have to learn to be unafraid of elephants. As much as I disliked the idea of shooting them, it was my job, and the more efficiently I could do it, the better and safer it would be.

Ten minutes later the trackers stopped. One held up his hand to indicate with his index-finger that the elephants were ahead of us. I took my rifle from Msatero and slowly, and as quietly as possible, opened the bolt and slipped a cartridge into the breech. My knees were knocking and the chest pains increased as, with one of the trackers, I moved forward to where the elephants were standing. The other natives remained behind to avoid making unnecessary noise. We moved forward slowly and steadily, and eventually some 100 yards ahead we could see the herd feeding on the lush green grass. Fortunately the grass was short and the area comparatively open. I remember looking at the trees to seek out the biggest to hide behind should the elephants charge.

At 60 yards I raised the rifle and selected a large bull. The tracker hinted that we should go closer. I thought him rash, but we crept closer and closer, and at about 40 yards I stopped and indicated that I was going no further. The elephants were milling around; I selected the one closest to me, raised the gun, aimed at what I thought was the brain, and fired.

Great confusion followed. The elephants screamed and trumpeted with rage. I turned and legged it back through the bush, closely followed by the tracker. The pain in my chest had disappeared; all I wanted to do was to get away from the place as quickly as possible, for I was convinced that we would all be killed by the huge beasts. By the time we got to where we had left the others, they too had taken to their heels and were already several hundred yards ahead. For them, as well as myself, discretion was the better part of valor.

When I saw we were not being chased, I stopped and took stock. I was not sure whether I had killed or only wounded the brute, and dreaded the thought of having to follow a wounded elephant through the bush alone. We stood silently for a few minutes.

In the distance we could hear the rumbling noises of the nervous elephants. I plucked up courage and went back to see what had happened. I fired another three shots

Bush clearing at Chipangali — one of the methods of eliminating tsetse flies

into the air, hoping to frighten the herd. We moved in closer and closer. In the grass I could see the huge bulk of a dead elephant, and I sighed with relief. We crept nearer and I fired two more shots in the air, which were, I discovered, unnecessary as the other elephants had long since left.

What a pitiful sight to see such a vast mass of what had been living flesh, now lying dead. Though I comforted myself with the fact that I had carried out my instructions, I was nauseated by the need to destroy such a magnificent animal. It had lived for dozens of years to reach its size, only to be felled in a split second by a single bullet.

Over the years that followed I had to shoot 71 elephants on control measures and in the tsetse-control area. I can say with sincerity that I am not proud of this, but I always killed as humanely as possible. I was ever-cautious of elephants at close quarters, and never really trusted them; of this I am not ashamed to say. If you lose your fear and respect for the great beasts, they will eventually be your conquerors. I lost a very good friend because of this fact.

Although I loathed the game-elimination policy as a means of tsetse-control, there was nothing I could do to alter it. I instructed all hunters to collect as much material as possible from every animal shot. They collected the skins of all animals (except buffalo and eland), the skull, any fetuses and parasites.

Small bijou bottles of preservative were issued to each hunter. When a hunter shot an animal he would at once collect as many ticks, or other external parasites, as possible, and place them in the bottle. This was labelled with the date, species, sex and locality. Later I re-labelled all specimen bottles with a resistal label and India ink.

After the animal had been skinned, the skin was salted and dried. If it had been pregnant, the fetus was collected and preserved in formalin. A large 10-gallon milk can full of formalin of the correct concentration was placed at each camp, and fetuses were stored in it. I made regular visits to all the camps and gathered all the material. I must have collected at least 2,000 fetuses, representing dozens of species. The skulls of animals were most important as it was from the skull that one could assess its age.

Then a request came from Graham Child, who was at that time keeper of vertebrates of the National Museum in Bulawayo, for the pelvic girdles of animals shot. This put an extra burden on the staff but I was only too willing to help; I hated to see the research material being wasted. We collected thousands of skulls, many hundreds of skins and pelvic girdles, and many other specimens. Whenever possible I measured and weighed the animals shot, and by the time I left Zambia 10 years later, I had recorded data on more than 2,000 animals, including the full weights of over 50

Game fence line in the
Chipangali area

African village and indigenous cattle in Chipangali area

elephants. The material was sent to various museums including the British Museum (Natural History). The scientific results of this work and the effects of game-elimination on duiker, kudu, hartebeest and other species, were published in scientific journals throughout the world.

About this same time I decided to do a detailed study of the common grey duiker, a species of which I was particularly fond. I have reared and kept many over the years. Thane Riney, an American Fulbright scholar working in Rhodesia, helped me a lot; he later joined the Food and Agricultural Organization of the United Nations. Thane was the finest of wildlife workers, a person I greatly respected. It was he who helped me with the aging of duiker skulls by tooth-development. Collecting every duiker skull I could find, eventually more than 900 were sent to the National Museum in Bulawayo. I would one day become the mammalogist of that museum and work on the very skulls I had collected in the field.

Over the years I also collected thousands of snakes and lizards for Dr. Don Broadley, keeper of herpetology at the Umtali (now Mutare) Museum. Later my paper was published on the snakes of the Eastern Province of Zambia, and another on the leopard tortoise of the same province. Also published was a survey of the reptiles and amphibians of the Nyika Plateau with an American zoologist, Dr. Margaret Stewart.

During my herpetological work I was bitten on the left hand by a puff adder — on the same finger bitten by the bibron adder many years previously. I injected myself with snake serum and immediately went to the hospital in Chipata. Although recovering rapidly from that bite, I was put out of action again a month later, this time by a large spitting cobra.

I was walking along the Lutembwe riverbed, which had only about six inches of crystal clear water in it, when I spotted a snake crawling into a pile of driftwood on the bank. I raced after it, and while peering into the pile of wood, a full jet of venom landed squarely in both eyes.

The pain was excruciating, like white-hot coals searing my flesh. Fortunately, I was next to the river. Unable to see, I stumbled wildly until I fell into the river. I plunged my face into the fast-flowing clean water and washed my eyes thoroughly for more than half-an-hour. The threat of total blindness entered my mind, for I knew how dangerous snake venom in the eyes could be. After a thorough soaking, I sat for a long time in the shade of a large sausage tree, finally managing to walk to my Land-Rover, a little over a mile away.

It was a terrifying, extremely painful but brief episode in my life. My guardian angel must have been watching, for without water so close at hand, my eyesight would have been impaired, if not lost.

44

Basket-making in the
Luangwa Valley of eastern
Zambia

Woll established African village in the Luangwa Valley

In spite of many bad experiences with snakes, I maintained a large collection at my camp at Kalichero, at one time more than 200 specimens, including a couple of rattlesnakes, a few water moccasins and a boa constrictor from South America. These were acquired from the New York Zoological Society in exchange for a few black mambas.

Also at Kalichero, I continued with my study of birds. After building a large aviary, I had all injured or orphaned birds brought to me. A large collection of waxbills and other birds were donated by a man from Lusaka who was leaving the country. I had lovebirds by the hundreds. The Nyasa (lilian) lovebird occurred by the thousands in the Luangwa Valley and along the large rivers. These were often caught, using birdlime, by the natives who pulled the main flight feathers out so the birds could not fly, and then took them to the larger towns and cities where they were sold for 10 cents each.

Hundreds of birds were confiscated by the police and Game Department and sent to me at Kalichero for attention. I washed the birdlime off the poor creatures, kept them until they grew back their flight feathers, and then released them. A number of bird study skins were prepared and sent to the Bulawayo and Durban museums.

One day while examining plants on a small hill, I discovered a chunk of rock about fist size, and very like iron ore. It was softer than iron, however, with various colors in it. Scratching around, I found several more pieces, and took them back to camp, where I already had an extensive collection of local minerals and samples. None of these specimens compared with my new discovery. A good friend in the mining business in the province sent a sample to the Geological Survey Department in Lusaka for analysis. He was convinced that the material was radioactive. Some weeks later he received a reply from the director of Geological Survey, part of which read:

> I submitted a sample for spectrographic analysis to Chartered Exploration and I have had an intimation this morning from them that both uranium and thorium are present, the former greatly in excess of the latter probably, although it has not been possible for the moment to determine quantitatively the thorium that is present. Other elements present in interesting or significant proportion are niobium and tantalum, magnesium and lead. There is also some titanium and minor amounts of other elements. The amount of radioactivity is about 40 times background.
>
> In regard to the position of the occurrence as you gave it to me, it would appear that it is mostly, if not wholly, outside the North Charterland concession. I shall look forward to having more information from you eventually when you have been able to examine this locality in more detail and any other specimens that you may find to be of interest.

My reply stated that I was not prepared to disclose where I had found the deposit until I had written confirmation that I would be paid "something substantial" for my discovery — if it proved economically and commercially worthwhile.

Back came the advice that "mining companies are not in the habit of paying out sums of money for every odd piece of rock or material put up to them." I therefore dropped the matter, and today my hill of "uranium and thorium" remains undiscovered despite the fact that many geologists have since attempted to find the deposit.

CHAPTER SIX

ORPHANS OF THE WILD

I WILL BE haunted forever by the image of that baby kudu with its crushed skull, brought into our Chipangali camp in 1954. The tsetse operation was quite ruthless. I hated the situation, and promised myself that whenever it was practical there would be no slaughter of young animals where I had control.

My staff was told that baby fauna were to be caught — not killed — and brought to the camp at Kalichero. In my ten years in eastern Zambia, about 100 young animals, including buffalo and elephant calves, were captured.

But feeding and rearing at this unusual nursery was often a heart-rending matter of trial and error, especially the experiments with feeding. Sometimes I was successful, but often my little charges died of diarrhea and dehydration.

Many times, by the time the babies reached me, they were very weak and agitated, and I became terribly distressed because of my early failures. Anyone who has nursed a beloved sick puppy or kitten, only to find it suddenly limp and lifeless, has an inkling of how I felt. Saddened and discouraged, I began to ask myself, "Is it all worthwhile?" After watching a young animal struggling for life and breath after days and nights of nursing, I wondered if it might have been better to have destroyed it when its mother was shot.

But I persisted. The human instinct to preserve the young and helpless is truly powerful. Overcoming my doubts, I again vowed to devote myself to saving these baby animals, to give them a chance to live. With many that I had lovingly reared and got to know so well, I knew that for their well-being they somehow had to be returned to the wild. But that was not a simple task. It was an exercise fraught with problems as complex as nursing and feeding, perhaps more so.

A young male kudu was released in the Luangwa Valley, many miles from humans, in an area where I felt sure it would be safe. I planned to camp close by for a few days. The next morning, to my utter dismay, all that remained of him were hooves and skull. It had been killed by a leopard. What the leopard had not consumed had been scavenged by vultures before I arrived at the scene. Their dark shapes were still there to mock me.

A second kudu was given to a farmer. It was six months old and I believed it to be out of all danger. Four days later, the farmer's dogs attacked it and tore it to pieces.

A pair of bushbuck were released only to be killed by tribesmen who saw them only as *nyama* (meat). These animals were unafraid of humans and had walked into a village, where they were immediately destroyed.

Monkeys and baboons were the worst to release. They became so used to humans that they nearly always made a beeline for any people they saw.

After many unsuccessful attempts, I decided to give up the idea. In the future my "proteges" would go to zoos, or to farmers who I knew would give them proper care. The first batch of animals went to a British zoo, where I hoped they would be content in their protected environment.

The then-governor of Northern Rhodesia, Sir Evelyn Hone, said he would like some small antelope for the extensive and well-fenced Government House grounds in Lusaka. I sent him six duiker and a pair of grysbok, and this worked out fairly well, except for one incident. One of the male duiker became so tame he would eat potato chips from the hands of Government House guests. One day he badly gored the hand of a housekeeper, and had to be destroyed.

Oscar and Chipera were two very tame warthogs, reared from tiny babies. They were real nuisances, and could be dangerous when around young children. I had to find a home for them, and a local farmer volunteered. He built a suitable enclosure out of pig-wire, and the warthogs were duly delivered.

That same day I had an urgent phone call from a very disturbed farmer. The hogs had broken out of their enclosure and were chasing his staff in all directions. "Will you please come immediately," he begged.

I drove to his farm, where I was confronted with a scene out of a comic opera. Natives in panic were sitting on the highest points they could find. Several were clinging to trees. A couple were perched on oil drums. One was on a tractor, and some were balancing precariously on fencepoles. Strutting about were two infuriated warthogs.

As soon as a victim tried to descend from his perch, the animals would charge and drive him up again. Because they knew me so well, the warthogs ignored me. I filled a tin can with dry corn and began to shake it. As the maize rattled, unmusically, the warthogs followed, right back into their enclosure.

Unfortunately, they became an increasing nuisance, continually breaking out, and, I regret to say, they too had to be destroyed.

As I watched my beloved animals gradually die from various causes, or saw them sent off to zoos thousands of miles from their natural environment, my thoughts turned to the need for a wildlife orphanage. There they would not just be passed on from person to person, be killed for food, or be destroyed if they became a pest. This would not only be a haven, keeping the animals safe from predators and other dangers, but it would also provide an invaluable research center.

At that time it was only a dream, but a vivid and persistent one. Unlike so many dreams, however, this one would be fulfilled, but only after years of sunshine and shadow in my cherished African bush which gave me each day new adventure — and new knowledge.

As more and more people learned of our animal nursery, I became the Gerald Durrell of Zambia. Apart from those animals my staff rescued, others began to flock in from far and wide, brought by people hoping to save them. I made a firm rule from the start: I would not pay for animals — not from miserliness — but because the alternative meant people might trap them deliberately for sale. Many of the young animals brought in were found when natives were clearing their lands of bush getting ready to plant their crops.

One day a farmer arrived with a basket containing a newly born animal which he called *Nyalubwe* (leopard). Looking at it, I could see no resemblance to a leopard. It was a very dark color, with none of the typical rosettes. It had dark spots, small ears and its eyes were still closed. I had never seen a newly born leopard, and I loved the little creature at once. Though he could not see his "enemy," he growled and spat ferociously as I removed him from the basket. I named him Chaka, after Chaka Zulu, the famous king.

Chaka (the baby leopard) had been born in a cave not far from Kalichero. His mother had raided a nearby village, killing some goats. After eating her fill, she returned to her lair. Next morning the natives followed her spoor, and as she bolted out of the cave, they shot her. Of the two little cubs in the cave, one was killed by dogs as they rushed in, while little Chaka was saved for me.

At first it was a struggle to feed him, but after a couple of days we had him contentedly drinking goats' milk, and he soon started putting on weight. Within four days his eyes had opened, and what eyes now surveyed me! From their clear, cool, grey depths, with glinting, yellow streaks, he looked at me, sometimes quizzically, often challengingly.

He was always a courageous cub and would often claw and bite me. From a very early age he became quite fearsome. It was more a case of being over-boisterous, and most of the scratches and bites I suffered were due to his rough play rather than an intent to harm.

Not long after I acquired Chaka I flew to Europe for an extended vacation and left the leopard cub with Dick Hyan, a veterinary officer in Chipata. By then (March 1961) Chaka was two months old. He had a beautifully glossy coat and well-defined rosettes on his golden-yellow body. His snow-white belly had distinct black spots. The black and white stripes on his coat were very clear, setting off to perfection his immaculate white chin. He weighed 7½ pounds, and when I collected him five months later he was already a sizable 40 pounds. It was difficult to handle him so, although his dignity was obviously offended, we employed a collar and chain. He had to be caged during the day but I took him for a walk each night.

As time passed Chaka became more and more a problem; when he jumped on me, he tore my clothes to ribbons. He would hold on tightly with his teeth and frequently draw blood, even though he was only playing. At 11 months he weighed 65 pounds and could still be handled on a chain and collar. It was a most uncomfortable experience, however, because he was so ferocious when he played. A few weeks later he was put permanently in his cage, not to be handled again.

Chaka turned out to be one of the most beautiful leopards I have ever seen. His coat was soft and bright yellow. But he was a most independent animal. In October 1962, when just 20 months old, he severely bit one of my staff on the arm. Morrison Chagomera had put his hand through the wire of the cage to stroke him and Chaka grabbed him. The more Morrison pulled, the more the leopard pulled with both teeth and claws. He finally drew the entire arm into the cage, ripping off much of the flesh. Morrison was flown to Lusaka Hospital where for many weeks he underwent skin graft operations. He suffered a great deal.

Although I loved the leopard, I had no alternative but to destroy him.

And then came Sheba, a female leopard and one of the most outstanding animals of my nursery. When I got her from a native on 28 January 1962, she was about 10 days old. Her eyes were already open, but still opaque. She weighed 2.2 pounds. She grew fast, and by the time she was eight months old she turned the scale at 34 pounds. When a year old, she could still be handled with ease, and although wonderfully tame with me, she could not be trusted around other people.

Sheba fed from a baby's bottle with a normal-sized teat. At three months she could climb trees with ease, dragging large pieces of cloth up with her. If she was given raw meat from the butcher, she would be tame and manageable and I could handle and stroke her. But her whole attitude changed when she had a mouse, a dove or any natural food. Then she was extremely dangerous and would attack without hesitation.

Even when they are not feeding, leopards are very unpredictable. One minute Sheba would be loving and playful, and the next ready to bite and attack. She followed me about like a dog. If I ran she'd try to keep up with me. While riding in the Land-Rover she would usually sit quietly beside me, but occasionally she would leap suddenly on my shoulders and bite me on the neck. It was unpleasant and painful, and not calculated to help the driver's concentration!

If I felt the warm blood trickling down my neck, as sometimes happened, I'd give her a good hard slap, then stop the vehicle until she calmed down, for she became aggressive and nasty — a most uncooperative passenger.

Her favorite game when out walking in the bush was to stalk me. Then, from about ten feet away she'd charge and jump onto me, often tearing my clothes and leaving long bleeding scratches down my body.

All this time I was training her to kill for herself, and she was released in the Lukusuzi Game Reserve north of Chipangali when she was more than two years old.

In late 1961 a wonderful pet — a baby serval about 10 days old — was brought to camp. His captor had been clearing grass for a new maize garden when he disturbed an adult serval. He found a single male kitten hidden in a nest in the tall grass. It had a long, fluffy, soft coat — a pale sandy-brown color — very closely spotted over the dorsal surface. His eyes were open but he could not really see well. The little ears were already erect, very black, and with a dull, dirty-white crossbar. The facial pattern was not clearly marked, and there was a bare patch on either side, between the eyes and nose. The little chap's teeth had not yet pierced the gums.

At four-and-a-half months he was beginning to look like an adult animal, a beautiful, golden-orange, with clear spots and stripes of pitch-black. He was completely tame and roamed free at all times, wandering around like a domestic cat. He slept on my bed at night and purred loudly, but did not like to be handled or picked up. By the time Snookie, as we called him, was eight months old, he was killing poultry and anything else he could get hold of; as a result our chickens and ducks had to be securely locked up. At a year he was still completely free, but he spent most of the time outside. Shortly thereafter I sent him to a zoo, for I was afraid he would be killed by other predators, dogs or even by humans.

The female genet will often have her young in a hollow tree or a hole at the base of some large tree. These trees are often felled by natives when bush-clearing, and only when the tree hits the ground do the young genets emerge. Over the years many litters were brought to me and adopted. Genets are easy to rear but not suitable as pets. They are excellent climbers, and as kittens they love to scramble up curtains.

We had a lovely domestic cat named Tinkey which was lactating when two genet kittens were brought to us. The kittens were given to her and she loved them and reared them without difficulty. Both genets had the run of the house and eventually left of their own accord. I like to think that they survived in the wild. I released several others in the years to come, but only when I was sure they could look after themselves and could catch their prey without difficulty.

You can imagine the excitement when we "adopted" our first baby elephant. Some baby! Although she was less than six months old and not quite three feet high, she was full of vitality and character, as we soon discovered when we set out to bring her to Kalichero.

It all began when one of my game guards ran into camp one afternoon to report that the tsetse-control hunters had shot two elephant in nearby hills. One was a female with a very small calf. He said the baby was *Abwino kambili* ("very nice indeed") but also very fierce. Whenever the hunters approached the dead elephant the baby would charge and drive them off.

It was routine orders by this time that baby animals were not to be killed. This particular baby, however, had proved much too wild and big for the hunters to handle themselves. They said it was a very dangerous beast and they were all afraid of it. However, the game guard added, since I had *makwalo* ("magic medicine") he felt sure it would be no problem for me to capture the youngster. It was comforting to find that my staff had so much faith in me; I could not let them down.

Morrison and I, with four assistants, piled into the Land-Rover and set off down the winding dusty road at breakneck speed. We covered the first 10 miles in 10 minutes. Then we had to go "bundu-bashing," crashing our way through grass as tall as a man in places, bumping over rugged broken terrain, and finding where we could ford the numerous streams. The heavy rainy season (it was January) was upon us and the ground was often soft and muddy. Sometimes the vehicle sank in and had to be manhandled out, even with the four-wheel drive.

Serval cat, one of the orphaned animals that came to the camp in the Chipangali area

At last we reached the place where the elephants had been shot. But what had become of the hunters who had been left behind to watch the baby elephant? There was no sign of them. Then we heard some shrill whistling which appeared to come from a sausage tree. A sausage tree has strange pendulous fruits like gigantic brown salami, and there, hanging precariously among the sausages, were the two hunters who had, as was soon evident, become the hunted.

When they saw us their relief was genuine. Grinning widely, they jumped down and ran toward us. There was no need to be afraid any longer, they announced, since the *bwana* had arrived. All would be well.

At that moment the elephant spotted us and charged. It was an alarming spectacle. Fanning out its ears and rolling up its trunk the "baby" came storming and screaming through the bush. The seven men at my side took off at panic speed, climbing as high as they could into the nearest trees, yelling all the while. There was a great hullabaloo.

Although the little elephant was only about as high as my belt, it was an astonishing sight as it charged, showing clearly that it saw me as an enemy and meant to destroy me. I stood my ground, for I was absolutely certain that it would stop before it reached me. Even if it didn't stop, it was too small to do any serious harm!

How wrong I was. The little dark bundle of hate came storming on like a small bulldozer. I opened my hands and stretched out my arms to receive the shock. I hit the ground with a thud — the surprise of my life. To make matters worse, she immediately spun around and charged again, screaming with fury. I did not wait to be knocked down again but, like my sensible assistants, took to the bush, much to their amusement. By this time they were all lodged much higher than necessary in the trees.

Luckily the calf did not follow me, but returned to its mother's body. It was pathetic to see the magnificent beast lying dead with its tiny baby standing guard.

After recovering from the shock, I approached the dead elephants, but this time from another direction, keeping the dead female between her baby and me. I managed to get right up to the mother before the baby took notice. As it charged I jumped onto the body of the mother. The little mite was still attempting to get at me.

It was obvious we would have to manhandle it and tie it up before we could load it on the Land-Rover. I yelled to my helpers to come, literally, down to earth, and to fetch a bundle of bark-rope to tie the baby's legs. This material comes from the bark of a *Brachystegia boemhii* tree, and makes excellent rope. With a great deal of noise and enthusiasm, they set about tearing at every tree in sight, and soon had enough bark-rope to tie up a dozen elephants.

56

After much charging by the baby, and yelling from the natives, we eventually had the little calf on the ground, holding it as its legs were tied together. I brought the Land-Rover as close as possible. Then came the problem of getting the 400 pound baby into the back of the short-wheelbase Land-Rover. After much heaving and shoving, eventually the grey captive was safely on board.

The return to Kalichero was completed without incident as we followed the tracks made by the forward journey. At times the front wheels of the vehicle were barely touching the ground as the seven natives, elephant and myself moved slowly along in the small vehicle.

We tied the baby up by one hind leg for the night. By the time we finished the sun had set; the little elephant looked very sad and out of place. Such a magnificent little animal deserved better treatment. It screamed and tugged at the rope all night and was almost exhausted the next morning.

At sunrise a gang was sent out to cut poles for a stockade and within hours the new "house" for Jenny (as we named her) was ready. In the stockade she screamed and stormed about, trying to get out.

The next problem was feeding. Pretoria Zoo recommended cow's milk and a gruel of cooked mealie-meal (cornmeal). The preparation of the mixture was no problem, but how were we going to get the food into Jenny's mouth? Any attempt to get near her was met with a charge and she made no bones about her intentions.

The day after her capture she ate nothing, refusing even to drink from a bucket. The second afternoon she tried to suckle from a canvas tarpaulin which covered half her stockade, erected to provide shade. I had a bright idea. From a canvas waterbag, I cut off one bottom corner and filled the bag with the food mixture. Where the tarpaulin sagged into the stockade, and where the calf was attempting to suckle, I cut a hole about three inches long. As soon as she tried to suckle, the tip of the waterbag was stuck through the hole in the canvas and presto — success!

She took to the canvas bottle at once and for the next week, while taming down, she was fed this way. A few days later she started drinking from a bucket, and the water-bottle feeder was dispensed with. Feeding her with a bucket was successful but slow. She would suck up a little milk with her trunk and then squirt it into her mouth, taking in about a pint of milk at a time.

After 10 days she was tame enough to be let out of her stockade and wander freely around the camp. I could have let her out earlier but didn't want to take any chances which might upset her. Abson Jumbe was chosen to be her constant companion.

He attended to her day and night, even sleeping with her. How he loved the job, and Jenny became lonely and depressed whenever Abson Jumbe had to leave her.

Daily at noon, when the sun was high and shining brightly, Jenny was taken a half-mile to the river for a swim and a washdown. I would walk in front, followed by Abson. Then came Jenny and Prince, my Alsatian, and sometimes even my donkey, Pegasus, joined the curious procession. Crowds of villagers would come to the river to watch Jenny take her bath. She became so tame and affectionate that the slightest squeeze would make her bellow with delight. The locals spread the word that the *bwana* at Kalichero had taught his elephant to talk to him.

At first Jenny didn't know how to eat leaves. To start with, she could not find her mouth. She would pick up a trunkful and search about with them until she finally found the spot. She was a wonderful animal and I grew quite fond of her.

But it was not all fun and delight. She often got a "runny tummy," and then for no apparent reason would become constipated, each time making her very weak. At times she was in good form and the young children from Chipata would ride on her back. Then a few days later she would be ill. She also suffered from weak back legs, and although she was given calcium and vitamins, they did not seem to help.

Jenny learned to open the front door of my house at Kalichero and would come into the lounge and lie down on the leopard-skins. Luckily I was a bachelor at the time. But tragedy was coming. After four-and-a-half months in captivity Jenny became weaker still and her hind legs gave her a lot of trouble. Then she caught pneumonia, and for a week she could hardly move. One dreadful day she just lay down and died.

She had been so gentle and so lovable. She left a great gap in our lives at Kalichero. It is hard to believe that people can become so deeply attached to an animal. The news of Jenny's death soon spread among the area people and hundreds called to say how sad they were. Many brought live chickens and green mealies as tokens of sympathy.

A few years later I acquired another young elephant. It happened that some tribesmen were collecting honey in a remote area when they found a dead female elephant. Suddenly a baby came charging out of the bush and sent them fleeing in all directions. I was camped about 20 miles away when I heard about it. The baby was very weak, and judging from the mother's carcass, she must have died at least four days earlier; the baby had been without food or water for that period.

Young "Bwalo" was much larger than Jenny, but we had no difficulty capturing and loading him on the Land-Rover. He was fed on undiluted cow's milk, but he

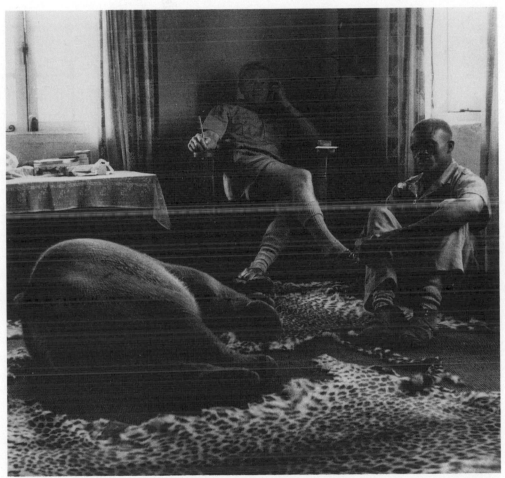

Viv Wilson with Abson Jumbe and the baby elephant Jenny

was too weak. The poor little fellow only lasted another two days. It might have been kinder to have shot him when first found, but baby elephants are such fine animals, I could not resist the chance to help him live.

There is sunshine in the wonderful African bush. But there are shadows too.

Author with road-building gang near Norman Carr's Lutembwe River Camp

CHAPTER SEVEN

THE LUANGWA VALLEY

THE WORLD OVER, the name of this fabulous land, Africa, is associated with big game, and Zambia is singularly fortunate in having on its doorstep a vast natural zoo. The Luangwa Valley is part of a geological formation known as the Great Rift Valley which stretches from the Red Sea right down to southern Africa. This tremendous geological fault virtually splits Africa in two. In the Great Rift Valley lie the Nile, the great lakes of East Africa and finally, the Luangwa Valley. It is about 2,000 feet lower than the surrounding plateau. It has a well-defined escarpment in the east, and in the west an unbroken range of mountains that stretches for hundreds of miles.

Mopane trees cover most of the Luangwa Valley. Mopane is heavy and exceptionally hard wood. The underlying soil is a tough, black, impervious clay. During the rains which last from November to March, the floor of the mopane veld is covered with soft, fine grasses which often grow in an inch or so of water.

As one descends from the Chipata Hills to the valley, the vegetation changes from *Brachystegia* woodland to mixed thickets, and from the *Combretums* to the true open mopane woodland. The scrubland of the hilly areas gives way to alluvial grasslands and woodland of the valley proper, the latter being much influenced by the dynamic behavior of the great Luangwa River which floods each year during the rainy season. The river winds its way down the center of the valley, and picturesque oxbow lakes and lagoons form during the rains when the river's banks are broken and the whole area is under water. Nearly every lagoon or oxbow lake is covered with green water-plants, colorful lilies and huge, shady trees, especially the hard, black-ebony trees.

The valley is probably the most prolific game area on the continent. In my travels in many countries of Africa I have seen no better. In the dry season, game is heavily concentrated and one need only walk for an hour or two in the morning to see a wide variety of species. In some places in the valley it is impossible to go far without meeting several herds of elephant, especially groups of young ones led by a weather-beaten old cow.

Buffalo predominate. They are found everywhere in groups, varying from five or six to herds of several hundred. Lion are fairly common throughout the valley, though not in such large numbers as I have seen on the Serengeti Plains in Tanzania. Camping at the Luangwa River, one would hear them every night and often see them in the early morning, including some very fine specimens. The Luangwa lion has a reputation for man-eating and many savage attacks have been recorded over the years.

The beautiful, gold-and-black Luangwa leopard is particularly abundant in the valley but because of its nocturnal habits it is rarely seen, except with the aid of a spotlight.

Of the antelopes, the impala is by far the most common and are to be found in the thousands. Puku, waterbuck, kudu, bushbuck, reedbuck and eland are often seen. Occasionally one comes across herds of sable and roan antelope, and even Lichtenstein's hartebeest. Duiker are not common in the valley but plentiful on the plateau.

There is hardly a stretch of water in the Luangwa Valley without its own school of hippo. They have increased tremendously since their protection many years ago, and they are now, ironically, being cropped in certain places. Their bellowing and grunting noises are heard day and night all along the river. Even away from the river itself, every pool that is deep enough for a hippo to submerge in will support one or more of these grotesque creatures. In addition, every stretch of water contains crocodiles and thousands of birds, especially crested cranes, waterfowl and plovers.

Cookson's wildebeeste is found nowhere in Africa except in the Luangwa Valley. It is fairly common in the Lundazi District owing to its protection. The beautiful and graceful Thornycroft's giraffe is peculiar to Zambia and they number several hundred.

As the dry season progresses (April to October), it becomes hotter and hotter in the valley, and water becomes scarce, with the inevitable result that the game concentrates around the lagoons and along the river itself. By October and November the place is literally alive with elephant and other species before the rains start in November.

The rainy season presents a completely different picture, and as the mopane country becomes waterlogged, so the game leaves the river for the surrounding country. Elephant and buffalo often move many miles into the foothills and the plateau, returning months later when all is dry again.

Puku antelope in eastern
Zambia's Luangwa Valley

Hippo in the Luangwa River near Luambe Camp

One day, travelling in the Land-Rover close to the Luangwa River, we saw a female impala suddenly spring across the bush-track, closely followed by a single wild dog. The dog quickly caught up with the impala, ripped open its belly with a single bite, and brought it down. Death was almost instantaneous. Within seconds the dog had torn pieces of flesh from the buck and then it stuck its head deep into the chest cavity, tearing out the lungs, liver and heart. When it had eaten a great quantity of meat, it walked off into the bush, leaving the carcass where it had fallen. I decided to stay and watch, and my partner drove on.

Soon the whole wild-dog pack arrived and scrambled for the food. They grabbed the impala from all sides and pulled and tore it to pieces. Within minutes there was only a pile of bones. I was about 50 yards away, filming the sequence, when suddenly the dogs turned on me. It was time for my Tarzan act again, but this time it was even more dangerous than the baby elephant incident. I raced to the nearest tree, yelling and shouting at the snarling pack at my heels, and swinging my camera around by its strap to prevent them attacking me.

They were within a few yards of me when I reached the tree, which I hurriedly climbed out of their reach. I was absolutely petrified, while the dogs showed no fear of me. I'm convinced that they would have killed and eaten me had it not been for my yelling and swinging camera. I was still in the tree, in a state of shock, when my companion came back for me.

———————

A dedicated team of game rangers and wardens worked in the Luangwa Valley. They opened up new roads and developed camps and other facilities. One of them was Norman Carr. His two tame lions, Big Boy and Little Boy, became world famous.

Norman had the lions at a camp named Kapani on the banks of the Luangwa, and I visited him often. One year when the rains commenced, we moved the lions to one of my camps on the plateau and I looked after them while Norman spent a couple of months in England. Responsibility for the two beautiful animals was an interesting, challenging task, but not easy. Meat was always a problem, but fortunately we were destroying certain species of game on the tsetse-operations, and so all available meat went to Big Boy and Little Boy.

———————

Marula-Miti was a famous, venerable elephant bull that lived near the Rukuzi River. He was unafraid of humans, and most of the people living within miles of the river knew him well. His left tusk was long and thin, and the other was broken in half —

66

Elephant bulls on a sand bank in the Luangwa River

a worthless piece of ivory with an ugly jagged edge. He never moved far from the dense thickets which grew close to the river, and during the dry season he, together with hundreds of other elephants, dug holes in the dry riverbed in their search for water.

He lived, fed and roamed the area alone, and at no time was he ever seen in the company of other elephants. He had one favorite spot — a large marula tree close to the river in an area where few trees grew. The natives maintained that all the vegetation had been cleared within a radius of 30 yards of the large tree by elephants that visited it to feed on the fallen marula fruit.

Marula-Miti, as he was affectionately known by all the locals, spent long hours under his favorite tree just standing and flapping his great ears to keep cool. He would feed on the marula fruits and the locals would also collect fruit from the same tree to make beer. He was docile, very, very old, friendly and well-known. Then one day something terrible happened.

Two white hunters from Lusaka visited the Luangwa Valley controlled-hunting area to collect a few trophies, and included in their licenses were two elephants. They had spent about four days in the area and shot several animals but had no elephants. Then they came across Marula-Miti and for some inexplicable reason shot him. He dropped dead within 100 yards of his favorite tree, and lay there while the hunters tried to find some natives to help remove the tusks. The tribesmen normally love elephant meat, but no one would help. They were disgusted with the hunters for having shot their old friend, and word soon spread that Marula-Miti was dead. The hunters had acted quite legally, but they did not know the elephant was tame and beloved by all in the area — one elephant that everyone knew.

Three days later the meat was rotting, and the stench could be detected miles away. Still no one would help with the tusks. On the fifth day after he had been shot, Marula-Miti's tusks were pulled out of their sockets and taken away by the chastened hunters.

That was not the end. Every native who passed the carcass of Marula-Miti would throw a stone on it, until the whole mass of dried skin and bone was covered with stones. Vultures and hyena had eaten much of the meat, but the skin, because of it toughness, was untouched.

Months after the incident I visited Marula-Miti's grave. There was a mound of rocks and stones, a strange and touching memorial to a magnificent beast.

———————

Not far from the grave I had a nasty experience with a rhino. I was trailing elephant in the dense thickets with two of my trackers, Wiwa Lungu and Msatero Mwale, when we heard a grunt behind a large, dense clump of bush. I was walking in front, following

Elephant bull pushing acacia tree to dislodge acacia pods

elephant spoor. Instead of moving forward to see what it was, I cautiously stepped a few paces back and stopped. Wiwa Lungu, crouching, crept forward toward the thicket. Without warning, a rhino stormed round the bush and knocked him flat. As the tracker rose to his knees, the rhino gored his shoulder and smashed his collarbone. Before I knew what had happened the rhino was off into the thicket and that was the last we saw of him.

Wiwa Lungu had a five-inch gash and was bleeding profusely from the wound. We carried him three miles back to camp, and then took him by road to a medical post, without any sort of painkiller. Wiwa sat perfectly still as he was stitched up. I then drove him 50 miles to Chipata where he was admitted to the hospital. The stitches were removed, and the whole wound treated and restitched. He spent two weeks in the hospital, and when he left was none the worse for the ordeal, and ready as ever to go elephant-hunting again.

On another occasion, while in a truck, we came across a large rhino bull. I climbed on the roof of the cab to get some camera shots of the animal. Suddenly the great beast came storming down on us. Lyn Birch, who was driving, revved the engine but the noise proved no deterrent. The rhino smashed into the front of the Bedford truck, knocking it at right angles to the road. It then sank its long horn through the front mudguard (fender) and tore it off, before running off into the bush with the mudguard dangling from its horn. The rhino shook its head, flung the mudguard into the air, and then disappeared. I was pretty shocked as I picked myself up from the ground where I had been thrown from the vehicle. We could not understand what had upset the rhino.

Unfortunately I had to destroy two black rhino on the Chipata Plateau some years after the incident with the truck. A large adult cow took up residence close to my camp at Lutembwe River and often charged the women and children there. Late one afternoon, the rhino rampaged into the camp, scattering clay pots and anything else in its way, completely unafraid of the people living there. I destroyed the animal the next day, because I feared someone would be killed. Rhino vary so much in temperament.

Then later, near the Lukusuzi Game Reserve we came across a female rhino standing in the shade of a large tree. As we approached, it ran off a few yards and stopped. Suddenly it swung around and faced us. My friend, John, got out of the Land-Rover and the rhino came charging at full speed. John stood dead still, hoping it would stop, but it came on and on. As it reached him he jumped aside to dodge it, but he was too slow. The rhino hit him with its shoulder and bowled him over. It stopped and stood over him, its horn held very low, ready to gore him if he moved. It was

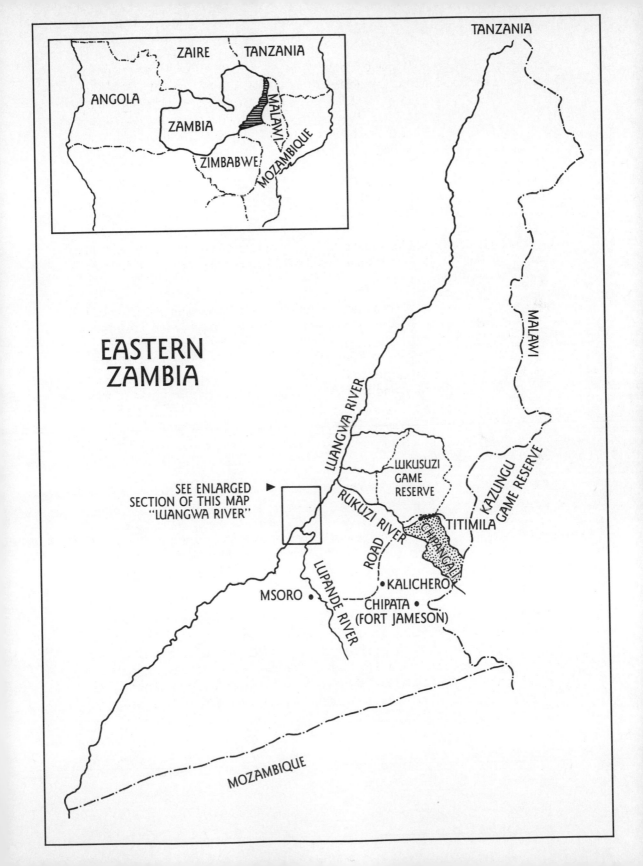

TANZANIA

ZAIRE   TANZANIA

ANGOLA

ZAMBIA

MALAWI

ZIMBABWE

MOZAMBIQUE

EASTERN
ZAMBIA

MALAWI

LUANGWA RIVER

LUKUSUZI
GAME
RESERVE

KAZUNGU
GAME RESERVE

RUKUZI RIVER

SEE ENLARGED
SECTION OF THIS MAP
"LUANGWA RIVER"

CHIPANGALI

TITIMILA

ROAD

KALICHERO

LUPANDE RIVER

MSORO

CHIPATA
(FORT JAMESON)

MOZAMBIQUE

a tense and anxious moment. I rapidly loaded my .375 Magnum rifle, took careful aim, and shot the rhino in the brain. It died instantly, almost dropping on top of John. Much subdued, we returned to Chipangali camp where we collected a gang of natives and a five-ton truck to bring in the carcass.

It proved to be a pregnant cow with a large fetus in its uterus. It also had the head of a spear embedded in its hindquarters. It had obviously been there for many years for the wound was completely healed.

———————

The late Johnny Uys, a senior game warden, was one of my best friends, and we had many memorable times together in the Luangwa Valley. One year we were instructed to take two Americans on a fortnight safari. They were entitled to shoot two animals each per day, and in due course they bagged their quota, including a beautiful lion and a fine leopard. One had shot a large elephant with tusks of 60 pounds a side. The other visitor was anxious to get an elephant as well, and one morning, quite by accident, we came across a monstrous beast.

I will never forget Johnny's face when the American said, "That elephant will be OK, I should like to shoot it." Johnny tried to persuade him to leave it. He suggested that he might get a bigger one later in the day. But Johnny had no luck. Without more ado the American aimed and fired, and the elephant ran off, wounded. We followed it and finally killed it. Its tusks weighed well over 100 pounds, each side.

What a tragedy it is when so magnificent and ancient an animal is destroyed. It had taken several decades to reach that size, and just to satisfy someone's hunting instinct, it is shot to provide a trophy and a boost to someone's ego. We were sick at heart.

I didn't like the safari business at all. Dealing with rich clients, I got the impression they felt they could bribe me to exceed their quota. One offered me a camera if I would let him shoot a second roan antelope when he was allowed only one. Often five pound notes were flashed around as "tips." I am not one to be bribed, least of all by hunters whose only ambition was to return home and brag of their "kills" in Africa.

More than anything, these hunters wanted to shoot lion, elephant, kudu, buffalo and leopard, and most of them shot all these species within walking distance of the camp. The camps were established at the river's edge, usually on a high bank, where one had a good view of the valley.

Those were some of the bad times. I was much happier helping with serious research. In June 1962, three members of the staff of the British Museum (Natural History), and one from the London School of Hygiene and Tropical Medicine were sent to the Luangwa to collect mammals (and in particular, ungulates), and to study their role as hosts of parasites and diseases. During their three-month stay they established base camps in three different areas, two in the Luangwa Valley close to the river, and the third on the Nyika Plateau.

I visited their camps many times and helped them collect the larger specimens, especially Cookson's wildebeest. These were the good times!

CHAPTER EIGHT

LIONS

IN MANY YEARS of high adventure, one day looms in my memory. I saw a pride — that word is well chosen — of 19 lions pull down a courageous old male giraffe. It's seldom one sees so many lions together, and although the battle with the giraffe sounds one-sided, the drama lasted several hours. And one of the lions was killed!

On TV screens or from the safety of an automobile, giraffe present a rather comic appearance. They are strange, graceful creatures. As one watches them, there's a feeling that a joke is hidden somewhere — because of that ridiculously long neck.

Make no mistake, a kick from one of those long powerful legs can be lethal. When Msatero Mwale and I came upon the scene near the Luangwa River early one September morning in 1956, one of the lions, a young male, lay dying, its back broken by a kick from the beleaguered giraffe.

The bull giraffe himself had several dreadful gashes on his hindquarters, and blood was flowing freely. But he was very much alive, and very angry. He lashed out with his hammerlike hooves if any of the encircling lions ventured too close. There were seven adult lionesses, four beautifully maned males, three adolescent males and four young lionesses. Nearby was the dying male.

The lions were cautious by now. And the old giraffe was still full of fight. The defiant old man lashed out with those terrible hooves when a lioness made a mock charge, but I could see that in the end he would have no chance.

One magnificently maned male, obviously the patriarch of the pride, appeared to be an impartial spectator. But the ferocity and noise of the other big cats in the attack was frightening. I had previously treated lions rather casually. From that day on I have had a healthy respect for them.

Suddenly, without warning, one particularly savage female made two gigantic jumps and landed squarely on the grand old fighter's back, avoiding the deadly hooves as he struck out at her. She dug her front claws deep into the giraffe's neck. Blood streamed from the raking gashes. Then she bit deeply into the neck.

The giraffe reared up like a horse trying to throw its jockey, but the great cat clung on tenaciously. Again the giraffe tried desperately to dislodge its grim rider. This was the chance the other lions wanted.

Two lionesses charged from the rear and tackled the giraffe's hindquarters. The weight of the lionesses hitting the giraffe while his front feet were off the ground threw him completely off balance. He staggered and fell.

The lioness on his back immediately moved her grip nearer the head and held it down. I was dumbfounded at the great cat's strength and ferocity. One male grabbed the giraffe's face and gradually but surely he engulfed the whole of the poor beast's nose and mouth within his and then held on, suffocating his prey. Another lioness bit deep into the jugular. The giraffe's struggles went on and on spasmodically, but growing weaker and fewer. His heroic struggle for life was over.

The spectator, the great male lion who had watched aloof, then deigned to join in with the coup de grâce. Finally, even the seven cubs emerged from hiding places and joined in — but they were looking for milk, not for meat. While the lionesses were tearing at the dead giraffe, seven babes were suckling away at their mothers' teats.

Lions and people don't mix. Every now and then someone gets killed and eaten, or injured by a lion. In May 1958 a lion entered a hut in an African village near Kalichero and killed a child, then mauled the child's mother and a man. The lion had pushed aside the reed door and then found himself trapped in the hut as the door closed behind him. I sent Morrison, one of my game guards, to investigate. While Morrison spoke excellent English, his ability to convey his thoughts in writing was limited. I think he did a fine job in his report:

> I am hereby submitting the incident report according to the information collected by me from the district messenger whose wife and child had such a fatal accident.
>
> The man stated that he made friends with a certain villager in Chief M'nukwa's area, this person has been staying at his garden as he was a business man.
>
> The business man called up his friend the district messenger for a visit owing to the fact that the messenger had no time for a visit to Chief M'nukwa's area he therefore sent his wife to go and visit the friend and his family. It was on Wednesday 14 May they were all happy to meet and share their talk and they arranged their last day to be on Tuesday this week. But on Friday 16 instant at 12 midnight, the lion visited the poor farm and actually it went straight away into a hut where the stranger and one of the family owners were sleeping; when he entered first

Adult and young giraffe give the photographer a once-over

there was no harm; but the woman (the stranger) heard a noise of a door when the lion was entering in and the door being closed back by itself therefore the woman mistook it as a dog as she thought.

"You see my friend there is a dog inside here, it has entered through under the door"; and before her companion replied her the lion took a chance of finding out a supper for himself; and at the same time he jumped and caught the child and by doing so the mother realized that there was a great war going on inside there and of course she found that the only child of hers was under the control of the brute of which the mother rejected the control and there rose a tug of war between the brute and the woman. She therefore cried for help, and also the other woman cried for help as well, and the old man came out and he then entered the hut and found that the woman had been badly mould up, by the brute. Then the man took hold of the brute by the tail and called his son for a shot at it so the boy brought a short gun and gave the brute five rounds so that was the end of the brute himself.

The man received two cuts, one behind the shin and the other one on the arm. But the woman had all her arms been eaten up and nearly cut off. The child was killed by the brute at the same spot. So the matter was reported to Chief M'nukwa who sent for the District Commissioner at Fort Jameson so the District Commissioner sent for the unjuried people to be taken to hospital in Fort Jameson where they are receiving treatment at present. The District Commissioner also sent the skin which is now at Boma yard well salted there.

The messenger is having a great doubt to whether his wife will recover from those wounds for she has got very serious ones on both arms and some along the leg.

He states that it was a very old lion having broken teeth and looked very very thin. It also had some pokepine's pricking hair found all over in it's body.

We collected some other news last night; another lion visited the messenger's quarters in Fort Jameson. But it was all lie for the one who cried for help was over drunk and he could only call for a help when he saw a dog coming near him then he said to other people please do come for a help for a lion wants to catch me. So some of the armed men went out and found that he was drunk and he was calling for the dog.

These are the only information I collected yesterday when you sent me to go and investigate for the proof of this matter.

MORRISON
H.T.C. GUARD

As Morrison's report indicated, the lion was very old and was suffering as a result of porcupine quills embedded in its body. No wonder it was so aggressive.

Once a lion becomes a man-eater it causes endless trouble. Sometimes whole groups of villages have to move. Man-eaters become very cunning and difficult to kill, and it is virtually impossible to get them to leave their hunting area. Several times I had to track down and destroy lions that had taken to killing domestic stock. Such punitive exercises usually happened during the rainy season when the grass was long and visibility poor, making the job doubly difficult.

The lion of Africa

. . . and his lioness

One lion I shot near Kalichero had eaten a native child, leaving, as gruesome evidence, a few pieces of cloth. The lion had eaten even the shoes, and when I destroyed it a couple of days later the undigested shoes were still in its stomach.

I had many experiences with lions, not only in the Luangwa Valley but on the plateau as well. I abhorred the job of tracking and destroying them. They were so cunning and fast that they were always difficult and dangerous targets. To hunt a lion in open country, where you can see it, is an exciting experience for any man. It is a different story when it takes to the thickets and long grass which it prefers. Its uncanny skill is then matched against your own in an environment which favors the lion.

I don't think I was a good enough hunter to enjoy lion-control, or, for that matter, leopard-control. Natives often asked me to shoot leopards that had killed their goats, poultry or even dogs. I assisted whenever possible and destroyed about half a dozen, but these tasks always meant sitting up for hours at night near a carcass waiting for the leopard to return. There was never an ounce of pleasure in it.

CHAPTER NINE

ELEPHANT MEAT

ALL TOO OFTEN an elephant herd wandered too close to villages, resulting in the destruction of food crops and even huts. The native leaders naturally called on the game officials for help. One such case in 1959, although starting out as rather routine, became so involved with mishaps it was almost humorous. And except for some mighty good luck, the incident could have ended in tragedy.

It had rained constantly for more than a week in late January. We received word that elephants had raided a village near the Mpomwa Hills in Zambia several times in the past month — the last visit only the day before. My job was to track the herd and kill the leader, in hopes the animals would move on and not return.

Upon arrival I recruited three trackers and, along with the village headman, we set off on the trail. The soggy ground made tracking effortless, with the path leading directly to and across the Lutembwe River. It was not deep, but extremely muddy and flowing swiftly. We managed to wade the waist-deep water and continued on the trail for about 10 miles — a trek that took several hours.

It was shortly after noon when we found the herd resting under a large baobab tree. Moving in closer, I counted 14 adult elephant. One large cow I judged to be the leader. Taking careful aim, I gently squeezed the trigger on the .375 Magnum and fired. The cow collapsed on her knees, then fell with a resounding thud. The herd was in utter turmoil, milling about with trunks high and ears flapping. They did not move off, however, because their leader was dead.

The wind was in my favor as I stood motionless behind a large tree. My companions were about a hundred yards behind me. I stood quietly, listening to the rumbling of elephant tummies, and thinking that time was beginning to be a problem — we were so far from the village and the Land-Rover. I could delay no longer, so I quickly fired three shots in the air. The elephants took off for the hilly country, crashing through small trees and bushes, screaming wildly in their stampede.

The natives were delighted at the sight of such a huge windfall of food, and were quite unconcerned that it was getting late in the day. They started skinning the elephant at once, apparently planning to carry back as much meat as they could carry. The whole village would return the next day to get the rest. About 2:00 P.M., with each person laden with 40 or more pounds of meat, we set off for the Lutembwe.

We reached the river a couple of hours before sundown, only to find it in full flood, a raging torrent. Large trees were being swept along, with other debris of every description. Bobbing up and down, turning over and over in the flood, was a drowned adult male kudu, its beautiful horns shining as they dipped in and out of the water.

I sat on the wet ground to ponder our predicament. There was no way we could cross such a strong current, and the river surely would not drop for many hours. The natives were babbling back and forth; each had some brilliant suggestion to offer. After working with these people for a couple of decades, I'm frequently struck by their marvelous sense of humor. Here we were at the river, with no possibility of getting across, and they showed no signs of depression or frustration. In fact, they all thought it a great joke.

While I didn't fully share their relaxed attitude, I knew that I just had to make the best of the situation. There was a flurry of activity as we prepared a shelter of bushes and grass tied together with bark-rope. It turned out to be a cozy little hut, and after a meal of roasted, or rather burnt, elephant meat, we sat and talked by a raging fire before turning in. Bed was a pile of green, damp grass, and we cuddled together. Warmth was the only comfort; there was a neverending succession of belches from my companions, with the repetitious smell of elephant meat.

At 3:30 A.M. I had had enough and got up to put more wood on the fire. I sat there until the sun rose, and would have given anything for a steaming cup of tea or coffee. Little did I know that it would be many days before I would enjoy such luxury.

Breakfast consisted of more burnt elephant, and muddy water. The river was still high, so we decided to return to the carcass, cut it up and dry the meat there. On the way we happened on a flock of guinea-fowl, and I was determined to have one for my next meal. The mere thought of eating burnt elephant again, at least in the near future, made me shudder.

I had heard that game birds could be shot with a large caliber rifle by placing the bullet into the ground close to them — the theory being that soil and small stones would fly up and stun or kill the birds. I tried. The birds simply flew off. I followed them and finally got another shot, this time directly at one. The .375 bullet blew the creature in half. I picked up the pieces.

When we reached the elephant carcass, two men started to cut up the meat while the others gathered wood for the fire and long poles to make a drying rack. I made a small fire, plucked what remained of my bird, and was soon enjoying a delightful meal of burnt guinea-fowl!

By the time most of the meat had been removed from the elephant, its large belly, still unopened, was very bloated and beginning to smell. One of the natives pierced the outer membrane to allow the gas to escape. His intentions were proper but the application wasn't. He cut too deeply into the tissue and punctured the stomach.

Just that quickly the natives standing nearby were covered with muck that gushed forth with a frightening force. The stench was horrible, to put it mildly!

The odor apparently disturbed the bees in a nearby hive. Actually, they were more than disturbed, they were downright angry, and they swarmed wildly around us. We beat a hasty retreat, and an hour later it was still impossible to approach the carcass.

I decided to leave my companions with their problems, and slowly returned to the river and the little hut. I spent the night alone, and had nothing to eat but a handful of sour wild plums that I had picked along the trail. These plums are common in the area, and popular not only with most species of animals, but also with the local people. However, for me at least, they leave a very unpleasant dry taste in the mouth, and without water the resultant taste is awful. Even so, I had a good night's sleep, completely covering myself with grass and leaves.

Next morning, with the river as high and wild as ever, I returned to the elephant. My friends had driven away the bees by building a fire with lots of green grass on it, creating a huge cloud of smoke. The elephant meat was by now all cut up and dried over the fire.

I walked to some hills a few miles away, and on the way back shot a male duiker. After skinning and cutting it up, I kept the hind legs for myself and gave the rest to the natives. They were delighted. As much as they liked elephant meat, all agreed that duiker was better. Late that afternoon we returned to the river; for supper I had grilled duiker and sour plums. A tasty meal indeed.

Two days later we were still at the river. The natives were now becoming agitated and restless. I had eaten all of my duiker, and was back on elephant meat, only now it was the dried variety — actually more smoked than dried. It's not too unpalatable . . . if you have nothing else.

Next morning, though the river was still high and flowing fast, I decided to try to swim it. After wrapping the rifle in my clothes and tying it to my back with bark-rope, I splashed naked into the water. The strong current immediately swirled me over and over; I was being washed downstream at an alarming pace. The bundled-up rifle was a terrible handicap as I was tossed this way and that in the swift muddy water. I wondered if my fate would be the same as the drowned kudu I'd seen several days before.

Down the river I went, battling all the while to keep my head above water. My lungs were beginning to fill, and each desperate breath was a streak of pain. Suddenly I was washed against the limbs of a tree that had lodged against the riverbank. The branches were tearing into my flesh and I could feel the warm blood washing over me. Clinging frantically to a larger limb, I slowly worked my body to the trunk and dragged myself along its length to some rocks along the bank. From there I crawled painfully into the long, wet grass, where I lay for what seemed like ages. My head reeled. I vomited brackish river water. My naked body was cut and bruised. I was thoroughly ill from exhaustion. How would I ever make it back to the village?

As I lay sprawled on the bank in a daze, I thought I heard voices somewhere in the distance. At first I thought it was a dream. Then it dawned on me that the voices were real.

When my companions saw me being washed downstream, they were convinced I had drowned and were in a frenzy of fear and indecision. None of them were proficient swimmers, so it would have been senseless to try to save me. They had followed the river bank, calling out while searching for my body. It was their voices that roused me from my stupor.

When they were opposite me, I fired a shot into the air, to show that I was alive. I had no energy to call out. They screamed with delight, and I could hear them chattering endlessly as I drifted back to sleep. When I awoke, I was cold, and shaking with a high fever. I had had malaria many times over the years and I was sure the recent days of stress and fatigue had brought it on again.

My naked body was covered with dry mud from the river bank. The mud was mixed with blood from the deep scratches on my arms, legs and body. After my sleep, however, I was able to stand and call to my friends. My clothes had dried, and I put them on. It was already late afternoon, and I knew I could never make it to the village on my own before nightfall. I shouted instructions to stay where they were until morning.

With no means to make a fire or shelter, I pulled piles of grass from the ground and collected as many leaves as possible to cover myself. Strangely, I was comfortably warm, but slept fitfully. When I awoke, the river had dropped more than 30 inches, but was still high and dangerous.

The natives, however, decided that they must cross over. They left their bundles of precious meat hidden high up in some fig trees, then entered the water close to where I had splashed in. The river was a lot kinder to them, or else they were better swimmers than I thought, for they all made it without any mishaps.

A couple of hours later we proceeded slowly back toward the village and my Land-Rover that we had left seven days previously. It had been one of the roughest trips of my life, and one I should not want to repeat.

Unfortunately, I did suffer a serious bout of malaria and spent several days in Chipata Hospital. But being young and energetic, I recovered rapidly and was soon well enough to return to my exciting and unpredictable job. I guess some people never learn!

———

One day soon after this episode, a local tribesman from a village near Kalichero came running into our camp, urging us to come and see the "miracle" at his home. A tree had fallen to the ground and then stood up again of its own accord, he said.

This is what we found: The ground had become sodden from heavy tropical rains. On the banks of the river at the edge of the native's maize garden grew a fairly large tree with a canopy of foliage and branches. The tree grew at a slight angle and the weight of the wet branches and leaves had caused it to fall. The villager had lopped off the branches and foliage, for it was laying in his garden. When the trunk was relieved of this great weight, the roots still had a firm enough grip in the earth for the tree to slowly right itself.

The tribesmen witnessing this phenomenon were sure that an *imfiti*, a spirit in the tree, had caused the miracle, and they stood around in awe. I explained in ChiNyanja what had happened, and their relief turned the whole occasion into a great joke.

———

I once worked on a game operation for several weeks with a remarkable man who became a great friend — Rupert Fothergill. Rupert was head of Operation Noah — a unique project in which thousands of animals were rescued from rising waters and then relocated on high ground. The occasion was the damming of the mighty Zambezi River at Kariba Gorge, downstream from Victoria Falls, transforming an entire valley into a huge lake. The Kariba holds three times as much water as Lake Mead, above Hoover Dam, and the flooding of this vast area threatened every living creature there.

The task of moving all those animals in Operation Noah has been the subject of several books. I found the work very satisfying, and I made a 16mm film on the project, showing the capturing, weighing and measuring of dozens of animals. Some were netted or darted (drugged) and taken from the receding islands to the mainland shore and released. Others swam to safety.

Mostly we caught various antelope, warthog and bush pig. Sometimes we found tortoises and snakes swimming in the rising lake. Many half-starved monkeys and baboons, stranded in the tops of trees, were captured and then released miles away.

One day Rupert said it was time to capture a lone rhino we had seen on a small island; I knew this was not going to be a routine task. First we chased it on foot, but it always made quickly for the dense undergrowth, where a successful darting shot was impossible.

Finally we worked out a new strategy: We perched ourselves in a tree over a path the rhino used frequently. Our gang of laborers then chased the brute from one end of the island to the other, until at last he passed under us. He was darted from about 30 yards away in the right flank with a shot from a Capchur gun. Only one dart was needed, for he showed signs of being drugged soon after receiving the injection. Within 15 minutes he could not get to his feet.

The next problem was to move the massive animal. We built a sled which consisted of two long mopane poles for runners, on which planks were nailed and tied. After maneuvering the sled under the beast, a thick rope was attached and our whole gang tugged the contraption to the water's edge, and onto a raft made with a steel and wooden frame, under which were fastened 18 petrol drums.

When it had been tied securely to the raft, and pads of hessian and grass had been stuffed under its head, the rhino was given an antidote to the darting drug. Its breathing increased rapidly and so did its reflexes. It started kicking and knocking its head on the raft. Fortunately the pads saved it from being badly injured. Raft, sled and rhino were then towed about six miles to the mainland, and dragged onto the shore. The rhino lay alarmingly still. A couple of large buckets of water poured over it had the desired effect, and within minutes it was on its feet, charging the sled and everyone nearby before it ran off into the bush, none the worse for its ordeal.

―――――――

Thousands of wonderful and not-so wonderful things happened to me during the 10 years I spent in the Luangwa Valley and the Eastern Province. I could fill several books with the experiences. However, when Zambia became independent in 1964, I could see that my days in that part of Africa were coming to an end. I was a Colonial Office civil servant and entitled to a pension and a "golden handshake" of $25,000 for "loss of career." The money was truly welcome, but I now had to find another job.

Tranquilizer is administered to a bushbuck ram during capture operations

Porcupine rescued from Zambezi flood waters

A porcupine is placed in a sack for transfer to the mainland

Young kudu bull en route to the mainland

The kudu is off-loaded for release on the mainland

One of the impala rams being carried to the rescue boat

Rupert Fothergill takes refuge on a raft from a charging rhino

Several interesting offers came my way: Training Africans at the new Tanzanian College of Wildlife Management; working in Uganda on a thesis on tsetse-control and game-elimination for a degree; or joining the research branch of the Department of National Parks and Wildlife Management in Bulawayo.

One of my sons needed special medical treatment at the time, and Bulawayo in Rhodesia (now Zimbabwe) offered the best chance for this. And that is where I went . . .

CHAPTER TEN

FIRST, CATCH YOUR RHINO

THE WORD "HECTIC" enters my mind when I recall events in 1965. Working for Dr. Harold Roth, head of the Research Department of Rhodesia's National Parks and Wildlife, was not only enlightening but also involved long hours. And he worked harder than anyone, always peering down a microscope or writing reports — long after others had retired from a hard day's work. Part of a "day's work" for me turned out to be catching rhinos!

As many black rhino as possible had to be captured in the area where the Sengwa River flowed into Lake Kariba. Rupert Fothergill was in charge, and my job included the recording of scientific and technical data and assisting in the transfer of the animals to Wankie (now Hwange) National Park. The region was truly primitive. The bush-track to Sengwa camp passed over countless tributaries of the mighty Zambezi. In the Batonka villages, the topless women bore bright beads on their necks and arms — a reflection of the dark "timeless age" a hundred or more years ago.

At camp I learned that Fothergill was still using the old Capchur guns. We spent several hours sighting them in, and out of six guns, only two were operable. At 20 yards, we could hit a 12-inch bullseye using a 10cc dart; at 25 yards, we had to aim 12 inches high to get the same result.

Here are extracts from my diary during the rhino operation:

June 1, 1965

At 8:30 A.M. we came across two rhino, sleeping. After preparing the drugs, Rupert crept to within 12 yards of one, and fired. The dart was deflected by a twig, and snapped in half, missing the rhino. Both animals ran off a short distance. Rupert loaded another dart, crawled up quite close to one rhino, and again fired. The dart stuck firmly into its hindquarters before it scurried away.

We followed the tracks for more than an hour. Often the trail was wiped out by fresh elephant tracks. Then we lost it entirely. We returned, and found the mate, but it bolted and was gone before we could get off a shot.

Rhino hunting is extremely difficult. With the ground covered with leaves and dry grass, tracking is virtually impossible. There is much game in the area, and we have to watch out for buffalo and elephant. It is hard to get close enough to dart rhino, and there are few large trees to climb in times of danger.

July 3, 1965
We found fresh rhino spoor at 9:00 A.M., and at 9:40 we caught up with a male. By 10:10 I was close enough to dart him. The arrow flew straight and hard. Instantly he swung around and broke the needle of the syringe against a bush before much of the drug was injected. He gave a loud snort and was away.

After a long trail, we caught up with the rhino at 11:00 A.M. By this time he was wide awake and obviously annoyed. He made a mock charge and we all raced for trees. A nearby troop of noisy baboons did not help soothe the rhino's temper.

Suddenly he bolted into the bush, and we followed, cautiously. However, we soon realized he was too alert to attempt a capture, so we left him for another day.

Returning to camp for lunch, we saw six buffalo close to a village, and fresh spoor of elephant and rhino near a lake. All at once we spotted a male bushbuck in the lake, battling to swim ashore. As we watched, he sank and disappeared into the weed-filled water. It would have been impossible to try to save him. Besides, there were plenty of large crocodiles about. Another tiring day and no rhino.

Our Capchur guns are almost useless. They have very little power. The average darting distance, in the bush, is about 12 feet. We spend hours stalking rhino, then creep close very carefully, only to find the gun doesn't work, or the dart breaks off after striking the animal, and it runs off. All very frustrating. I am surprised there hasn't been a serious accident.

July 5, 1965
Left camp early and soon found fresh rhino spoor. As we trailed the rhino, we passed five groups of elephant. One old bull charged Rupert. We nearly had to shoot it.

Finally we caught up with a lone rhino, a female. Rupert stalked to within six yards and squeezed the trigger. Nothing happened. The gas had leaked out of the Capchur gun. The rhino heard the click of the trigger. Rupert scampered up a nearby tree. The rhino was under the tree, and Rupert tried the gun again, without success. The rhino bolted into the thick bush.

Back in camp for lunch, we tested another unreliable gun. It might have been good enough at very close quarters.

In the afternoon we found two rhino. I chased them so that they passed through a narrow neck of land between two sections of water. Rupert was hiding there, and as the animals passed by, he darted one in the buttocks. We trailed them and after nearly a mile, they parted.

First we trailed, and found, the wrong animal. We found the darted rhino at 5:40. It was standing with its neck resting in a forked tree. We had caught our first rhino!

92

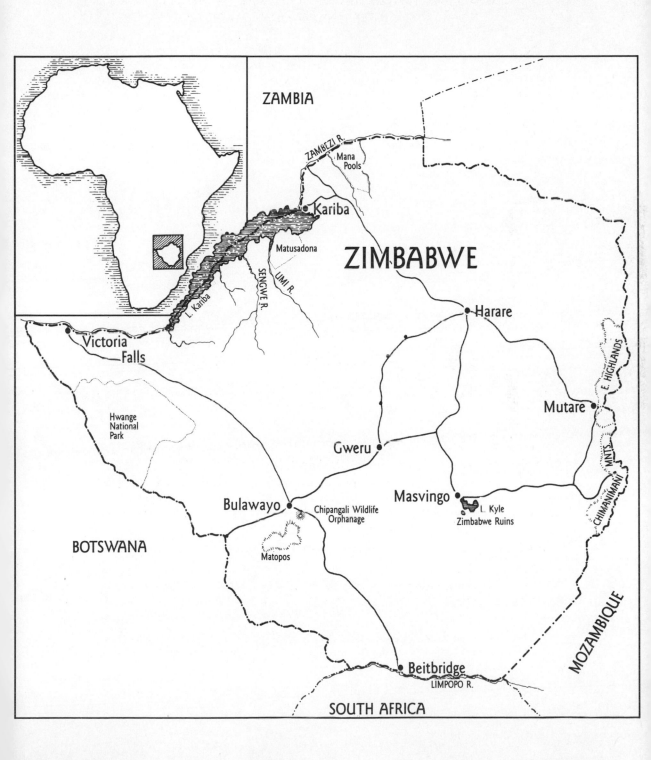

ZAMBIA

ZAMBEZI R.

Mana
Pools

Kariba

ZIMBABWE

Matusadona

UMI R.

SENGWE R.

L. Kariba

Victoria
Falls

Harare

Hwange
National
Park

E. HIGHLANDS

Mutare

Gweru

CHIMANIMANI MNTS.

Bulawayo

Chipangali Wildlife
Orphanage

Masvingo

L. Kyle
Zimbabwe Ruins

BOTSWANA

Matopos

MOZAMBIQUE

Beitbridge

LIMPOPO R.

SOUTH AFRICA

People at a Batonka village in the Zambezi Valley where rhino captures were being conducted

Family group at a Batonka village

Immobilized rhino being ear-tagged

Drugged rhino about to be loaded onto a truck

Chavuta means trouble in the local language. We named him Chavuta because of all the trouble he'd given us.

A road was cut to the rhino. With the aid of the vehicle lights and a lantern, we somehow managed to load Chavuta on the truck, and arrived back at the pens long after the dinner hour. Numbered metal tags were secured in each ear, with the same number branded on the horns.

The next few days were spent in camp attending to the captured rhino, and building new holding pens. Dr. Roth arrived with an English veterinary surgeon, and gave us a new drug called M-99.

July 18, 1965

We found rhino tracks at 7:30 A.M. One set belonged to a very small calf. While tracking, we stopped suddenly at the sound of branches being chewed. The distance, we discovered later, was 300 yards, and I was amazed the sound would travel that far. We stalked and darted the adult cow. The baby was lying about 12 feet away, fast asleep. The cow instantly charged and we ran for a large tree, reaching it in the nick of time.

The darted cow then raced into the hills, while Rupert captured the calf. It gave him little difficulty, although the screaming was deafening.

Rupert and the boys followed the cow, while the rest of us stayed with the calf. The cow was found a mile and a half away, in a dry riverbed. When the five-ton truck arrived, it took two full hours to load the huge rhino.

We carried the calf to the scene in a hammock, using a pair of native's overalls.

A few days after the above notes were written in my journal, I returned to Bulawayo, for I was scheduled to start a research project on domesticated eland. But the rhino capturing went on, with near disastrous results. As closely as I worked with Rupert Fothergill, my great friend, I could have predicted what happened shortly after my departure.

Rupert and a game scout were hidden behind a small termite mound, waiting for two feeding rhino to move close enough for Rupert to dart one. The men were so preoccupied that they did not hear or see a third rhino which suddenly appeared beside the scout, and directly behind Rupert.

The game scout shouted. Rupert tried to dart away, but slipped. The charging rhino struck him a glancing blow, throwing him to one side. A follow-up charge caught Rupert in the stomach. He was badly gored. Luckily the rhino ran off.

Rupert was flown by helicopter to a hospital in Salisbury (now Harare), where he recovered in several long, painful weeks.

But the capture operation went on, and many more of the great beasts were relocated in Wankie Park — including the one that gored Rupert.

CHAPTER ELEVEN

THE MATOPOS

ABOUT TWO BILLION years ago the granite of the Matopo Hills was formed, deep within the earth's crust where, very slowly, it began to cool. The molten granite was pushed up from the bowels of the earth, but was still covered by soil.

Millions of years ago the entire landscape of the Matopos, an extraordinary geological feature near Bulawayo, was almost flat. The present panorama of enormous, strangely shaped granite hills and boulders have been sculpted by eons of varying weather conditions. The soil which hid it after the original upheaval has been washed away by centuries of wind and rain. The Matopos have an extraordinary fascination; the precipices, canyons and caves are beautiful beyond belief.

Much of the Matopos is still undisturbed, retaining its natural wild beauty. By moonlight when great pinnacles of rock and massive granite domes silhouette the African skyline, their broken outline fringed by trees, they give a fairy-tale setting to a giant's world. The hills are even more awe-inspiring when tropical storms lash the granite, enhancing their ruggedness.

The Matopos begin 22 miles south of Bulawayo and stretch for 50 miles, with a depth about half that. A small section of the Matopos is a national park. If the region was all national park it would be perhaps the finest in the world.

On the smooth granite walls of the hundreds of caves and shelters in the Matopos are a great variety of paintings. The artists were the Bushmen, little people who lived in the area hundreds of years ago, and their art has given us a picture of the animals with which they shared their world, although it is unlikely that all the animals depicted actually inhabited the area.

One of the most startling paintings, in Nswatugi Cave, shows a white leopard. In other caves the walls display rhino, elephant, buffalo, lion, giraffe, cheetah and hippo. Some are exceptionally clear line drawings, and this remarkable, timeless exhibition includes many species of antelope.

There has been intensive hunting in the Matopo Hills for many years and today only the smaller antelope, duiker, klipspringer and steenbok, survive. There are some descendants of a herd of sable antelope. The wily leopard, with a plentiful supply of rodent-like dassies (*hyrax*) and klipspringer to eat, lives in the hills and caves.

Except for a small section of the Matopos, the bigger animals have disappeared. The exception is the game park. Animals have been re-introduced from other parts of the country since 1960, starting with five zebra and a small herd of wildebeest. Eland calves and giraffe were brought in a little later and gradually the park's animal population has increased.

The square-lipped (white) rhino is now well-established in the Matopos. In the second half of the last century Frederick Courteney Selous, the hunter and explorer, wrote that he often saw this species here. Other hunters, notably Thomas Baines, saw them as late as 1869, and one was shot (possibly the last) in 1896. Then, after being absent for half a century or more, a breeding nucleus was started with animals from the Umfolozi Game Reserve in Zululand.

One of my favorite animals is the little klipspringer which is found in the Matopos in the hundreds, if not thousands, on rocky outcrops and granite hills. They usually are spotted in pairs, sometimes in a group of three. Baboons and klipspringer are sometimes seen together at the same tree, the baboons in the tree, and the klipspringer below making full use of the wasteful feeding habits of the primates.

Young klipspringers keep well-hidden in rocky outcrops and venture into the open only when well developed. Klipspringers are distinguished from their antelope ancestors by their coarse, brittle hair. The adults as well as newly born young are eaten by leopards and pythons. There are records of black eagles feeding on klipspringer babies. And presumably servals and caracals also feed on them.

I recall one particular visit to the Matopos. I was making notes for a research project. Nothing had happened for hours; even the dassies seemed to have deserted the area. I was so bored that I dozed off, head propped against a rock. I must have slept for about an hour when, on waking, I was delighted to find some klipspringers on the rocky ridge ahead of me. They were unaware that I was sitting a few hundred yards away. Slowly, I raised my binoculars. There were two males and a female. One male's horns were only about two and a half inches long, the baby of the female. She was evidently in estrus, for the adult male was paying her unusual attention. Every now

Dassie (hyrax or rock rabbit) in the Matopo Hills — the main prey of eagles and leopards

White rhino in the Matopos — re-introduced into the area many years ago

and then, with stiffened front legs, he would paw her. This behavior is known to zoologists as "leg beat" — a sort of love tap.

The klipspringers moved slowly, nibbling a tasty bit of grass now and then. The young male walked toward a large, flat slice of granite, about a yard thick and about four yards long. On one side grew several clumps of the resurrection plant, which was at that time lush and green.

Suddenly, a leopard sprang at the young klipspringer and struck it with one of his powerful paws. The blow sent the poor klipspringer flying down the hill. It landed on a rock with a solid thud. It kicked and screamed, and tried to get to its feet. The other two klipspringers darted off, bounding from one rock to the next. In a few moments the leopard was on the young klipspringer. There was no need for haste. The little animal had both front legs broken, either by the fall or the original blow. The leopard, a large male, grabbed the helpless antelope by the neck, and gave a quick bite into the skull and neck. In a second the klipspringer was dead.

The leopard then sat quietly on his haunches and started to wipe loose the "quills" of coarse hair from his mouth. He was in no hurry to start feeding, and for some time he looked around as if to make up his mind where he was going to go to feed. Then he grabbed the klipspringer by the center of the back, and with its legs and head dangling, carried it up the hill. He dropped his prey, looked around for a couple of minutes, then settled down out in the open. He pulled out about ten mouthfuls of hair, systematically spitting each mouthful onto the rocks. It was the first time I'd seen a leopard feeding on a freshly killed klipspringer; it was interesting to see how he dealt with the coarse hair.

Five minutes later, he had still not started feeding. Once more he sat up and looked around — as if worried by being in the open with his prey. Suddenly, two pied ravens flew over him, making a tremendous din. That was the signal he needed. He picked the klipspringer up by its back, and walked over the ridge. After all this excitement, I poured myself a cup of hot tea. What a strange day it was: hours of boredom climaxed by half an hour's intense drama. Then nothing again.

That day, because I had had enough inactivity, I broke one of my rules. The leopard had left with the klipspringer an hour and a half before, and I decided I would see where he had gone.

It took 15 minutes to climb down to the valley and up the ridge where the killing had taken place, and from there it was easy to follow the route the leopard took. Loose hair had been dropped in several places, and spots of dried blood lay on the granite. About 160 yards from where the klipspringer had been killed, a clump of aloes, shrubs and a lot of grass grew among the boulders. The leopard had taken

Zebra in the Matopo Hills, near Bulawayo, Zimbabwe

his prey there, but there was no sign of him. A troop of baboons barked loudly in the valley beyond the ridge, and from the agitated sound, I guessed that they had seen the leopard.

Then I found the remains of the klipspringer. The leopard had eaten all the meat, the leg bones and hooves, and even much of the skin. All that remained was the skull, still with skin attached, and a large quantity of scattered hair.

———

Several months later, I was at another of my eight-hour observation spots, watching a group of dassies all huddled together. Although the sun was shining, it was not hot, and the dassies were trying to get warm after a long, cold night in their rocky crevices. Although half asleep in the early morning sun, they were still alert. Then one gave an alarm call. They all scattered to the nearest crevice under a very large slab of rock. When the dassies' excited chatter died down, I saw what the commotion and panic was about. A leopard, a young animal in prime condition, appeared. The dassies had wasted no time getting to safety.

But the leopard knew just where they were. He lay on his belly and peered into the crevice under the rock, and pushed his long front leg into the crack to fish out his breakfast. Then he tried another spot, where he again used his front paws to try to grab one of the frightened little animals. Then he stopped, sat dead still, and like a kitten, threw himself forward and tried again.

Alas, he had no luck, and after half an hour, looking thoroughly disgusted — and a leopard can look disgusted — he gave up and stalked off into the bushes. It was another hour and a half before the dassies dared to venture out, and even then, they were very nervous and did not move far from their haven.

The cunning and elusive duiker is the most adaptable of all antelope. He manages to survive where most other species have been eliminated. They are common in the Matopo Hills but, being nocturnal, are hardly ever seen. Only very occasionally are an adult male and female with a small baby seen together. Leopards and pythons are known to feed on adult duiker, as well as a host of smaller predators, including servals, caracals and jackals. Even the large birds of prey feed on newly born duiker.

Kudu are quite capable of jumping a game-fence, and so move in and out of the game park with ease. When I did my original survey of the large mammals of the Matopos National Park in 1968, very few kudu were seen, and only one had been introduced into the area. At that time I thought the population was no more than a couple of dozen. Today they are far more plentiful, and solitary males and small groups of mature females are often seen.

Secretary bird, occasionally kills and eats mammals, but its main foods are reptiles and large insects

Viv Wilson with immature black eagle — a species very common in the Matopos

I personally believe the habitat of the Matopos is generally unsuitable for giraffe and although they are often featured in the rock-art in the hills, I think that the painters had seen them in the acacia country beyond the hills, when out on hunting trips. Several giraffe have been introduced into the park since 1960 but they have either died, or met with accidents and had to be destroyed.

The Matopo Hills also support a dense eagle population, particularly the black eagle. It preys almost entirely on dassies. Val Gargett, a world authority on black eagles, says that there are at least 53 pairs in an area of 130 acres of the Matopos. African hawk-eagles, Wahlberg's eagles, martial eagles and many other raptors, representing a total of about 29 species, live in the area.

Gargett believes there are at least 190,000 dassies in the region. The black eagles alone probably kill 18,000 dassies in a year. One eminent biologist believes there are about 100 leopards in the Matopos. A leopard could eat at least one dassie a day and therefore 100 leopards would take a minimum of 36,500 in a year. Adding it up, about 54,000 dassies are taken each year by eagles and leopards, not to mention those taken by pythons and other predators. Using a 10 percent predation figure, there must be at least 600,000 dassies in the Matopos.

On five occasions I saw black eagles sweep low over the edge of exposed rocks on which dassies were sunning themselves, in an attempt to catch one, and three of the attacks were successful. The killings were rapid and clean.

One morning I watched a group of dassies fight for position in the first rays of the sun. They were so busy squabbling that they were off guard. Suddenly a black eagle swooped over the rim of the boulders, following the contours of the rock, and landed on one of the dassies. It screamed as the eagle sank its talons in. In a flash the rest of the dassies disappeared into their holes and hid among the rocks.

The great black eagle tightened its fatal grip and I saw clearly how he used his hind claws to stab the dassie to death. The hind claws are much longer than the front holding claw. In this particular case, the eagle squeezed three or four times, and the hind claws pierced deep into the thoracic cavity.

Seconds later the dassie was dead, whereupon the eagle, still holding its prey with one foot, looked around. Minutes passed before the eagle relaxed his grip. Before he did so, he pecked and pulled at the dassie with his beak as if to determine if it really was dead. He then fed for about ten minutes, tearing strips of red meat from the legs and body. Moving his head from side to side, the great bird then lifted the remainder of the carcass effortlessly from the edge of the rocky outcrop, and flew away into the vast valley below.

Leopards are common in the Matopos but because of their nocturnal habits,
they are very seldom seen

On another occasion in the Matopos, I was with a group of four visitors from Denver, Colorado, when we saw a secretary bird stamping at something in the grass. Secretary birds are noted for their incredible ability to kill snakes and then swallow them whole, so we assumed a snake was being stamped to death.

The grass was about 18 inches high, so we could not see what was getting such vicious and persistent blows from the bird's feet. We stopped our Land-Rover and watched quietly, but even with binoculars, we could not tell what was being hammered. The bird stopped his stamping and watched us for several minutes, but every now and then would look down at his prey to make sure it was dead. Then he would pound it again with another two or three blows.

Quite unexpectedly, he stalked off about 20 feet. We assumed he was going to leave his prey, but he turned around and returned to the "kill" and gave it another couple of blows. We waited patiently. He looked around and then began tearing at the carcass with his curved beak. At last we were able to see pieces of hair from the victim, and realized that it was a small mammal.

The bird went on plucking the mammal and once lifted it off the ground, and dropped it again. It was a small duiker, possibly newborn. For another ten minutes he played around with the little beaten up baby, occasionally pulling pieces of meat from the body. As the bird was obviously very nervous of our presence and we felt we had disturbed him enough, we drove on and left him with his most unusual prey.

———————

As the sun sets and darkness creeps over the rocky outcrops, the real Matopos comes to life. The first nocturnal creatures to emerge are the red rock-hares. They are plentiful throughout the hills and are exceptionally agile on the granite boulders. They can run up almost perpendicular rock-surfaces and jump several feet from boulder to boulder. I have also seen them well out in open plains feeding on freshly sprouted, green grass. When disturbed they bound toward the hills. In these open areas they fall easy prey to leopards and other predators, and even the great eagle-owls will feed on them.

I had a happy surprise during my research work in the Matopos with the discovery of the Cape eagle-owl, and was delighted when I collected a specimen in 1967. The discovery of the owl in the area was an eye opener to those who study systematics and ignore the ecology of a species. The scientist should always be prepared to expect the unexpected.

CHAPTER TWELVE

WILD PETS

YOUNG WILD ANIMALS constantly are taken into the homes of nature-lovers throughout Africa. In 1965, soon after my arrival in Rhodesia, I found I was forever collecting or releasing someone's pet back into the wild, or dealing with dangerous, unwanted animals.

One of the first was a lovely male reedbuck reared on a farm near Bulawayo. The owner found that his pet had developed a fine pair of horns and was becoming more and more dangerous as he became older. In fact, he had become a great nuisance, destroying the vegetable garden, chasing the dogs, entering the farmhouse, and even attempting to gore his owner. They tried to introduce the animal to the wild but he refused to stay in the bush, preferring the peaceful, domestic living conditions. He always returned to the homestead.

I was asked to collect the reedbuck and release it in the Matopos National Park. This sounded easy. After a great deal of trouble we managed to get it on the back of my Land-Rover. It had to be forcibly tied down. By the time we reached the park it was very tired, weak and distressed. After a couple of hours, however, he regained his strength, and began to butt my vehicle. It became quite aggressive. I was not happy about leaving it in the park, for I was sure it would meet with an unpleasant end.

It survived for a week on bread, cigarettes and other tidbits given to it by the public. It stayed close to the road, waiting for vehicles and begging food from the occupants. It had no fear of humans and I think it believed it was one. Then one day the poor animal was found lying by the side of the road dead. I was away at the time so we never knew the cause of its death, but whatever killed it, the incident showed that the creature could not suddenly adapt to a wild environment and to a strange new life.

Another incident, funny perhaps, but tragic, involved a young chacma baboon. A lady brought it to our office in Bulawayo. She had had it as a pet for more than a year. She said her husband had deliberately shot its mother because he wanted a young baboon for a pet. At first it was great fun and the whole family enjoyed the little animal. Everyone, including the neighbors, thought it funny when the baboon was destructive and dirty. But as it got older and larger, the funny side began to wear off. The family grew to dislike the baboon which they had so carefully looked after and taught all manner of things.

When they had to get rid of it they didn't know what to do. Nobody wanted it. I was instructed to release it on a ranch outside of Bulawayo. I protested, for I felt that it would soon die or seek human company. However, my boss insisted, so I did as I was told. I drove into the bush and set the little chap free. As I drove off it screamed and chased my vehicle. It jumped into the cab and sat clinging to me, refusing to let go. When I tried to pull it off, it urinated and defecated all over my clothes and neck. I had no alternative but to drive back to town with a stinky primate still clinging to me.

I was in a sorry mess when I got back to the office and in no mood for debates on the pros and cons of releasing baboons. I dumped the animal in the office and went home to bathe and change.

The little baboon was then sent to the National Museum. The geologist there, Craig Smith, was about to go to Diana's Pool, some 50 miles from Bulawayo, and he was asked to take the baboon with him and release it. As before, the frightened little creature, wanting nothing but human company, was dumped alone in a hostile environment to look after himself. Everyone was happy that the job was well done — but it was not the end of the story.

Next day a lady tourist and her husband visited Diana's Pool. As the car stopped, the lonely baboon made a dash for it and grabbed the lady around the neck, hanging on for dear life. The lady was petrified, afraid to move, thinking the baboon would bite her in the face. Since the baboon and the lady could not be separated, they were driven to the Bulawayo police station, where the officers eventually forced the animal loose. I was told the unfortunate animal was then destroyed.

A train of similar events can be traced with vervet monkeys. When they are young and gentle they are appealing and interesting around the house. Once they are adults the appeal lessens and they become a nuisance. Over many years, particularly in Zambia, I often tried to release monkeys and baboons. The experiments were usually unsuccessful. Animals should never be released near main roads, camps or places where humans can be reached. They always become a problem and finally have to be put away.

Paddy Wilson with young chacma baboon that would not go back to the wild

I once watched a beautiful young sable antelope get thinner and thinner and eventually die. As a tiny baby it was found on the Victoria Falls Road by a passing motorist, who brought it to the Game Department. I took the little fellow home and fed him on undiluted cow's milk for some weeks. When the time came for him to be returned to the wild, he was taken into the fenced Matopos Game Park and released. We hoped he would join with the other sable. The exact opposite happened. The wild sable drove him away and gave him such a rough time that he finally died of exhaustion and starvation.

I saw several other ex-pets die like this over the years and decided I would never try to release a "tame" wild pet back into the bush. I am not saying it cannot be done, for with proper facilities, and plenty of time, training and patience, one can succeed.

For me, the straw that broke the camel's back involved a group of young ostriches. The birds were about six months old, and as far as I can remember there were six of them. They were reared from chicks and brought to our office. I was told to release them immediately at Mpopoma Dam in the Matopos. I wanted to keep them in animal pens for a few weeks and then, once they were well adjusted, release them. However, I was overruled, and I released the birds as instructed. Confused, they ran directly into the dam and were promptly drowned. We loaded the little carcasses into the Land-Rover and returned to Bulawayo where we deposited the "evidence" at the Regional Office.

As the tragic toll increased from these many unsuccessful releasing operations I vowed that some day I would have my own private sanctuary. There I could keep, study and preserve animals that could not be returned to the wild. I often spoke about it to my superiors but the idea usually got a cool reception.

In 1968 I had the opportunity to fulfill my second ambition. There was a vacancy in the National Museum in Bulawayo for a mammalogist — as curator of mammals and head of the mammal department. I applied, and was given the post.

It was sad to leave the National Parks Department, where I had enjoyed my outdoor work, but I knew that in my new position I would be in the bush just as much, and I would also have the opportunity to visit foreign places.

CHAPTER THIRTEEN

DESERT, SWAMP & BUSHMEN

I JOINED THE museum on April 1 — All Fools' Day. Ken Jackson, one of the country's top TV hosts, asked me to appear on television to take part in a "scientific" April the First hoax. The scenario was that a German scientist had discovered an egg and a baby *Pterodactylus* in the Okavango Swamp between the Zambezi River and the Kalahari Desert. The pterodactyl, a flying reptile, has been extinct for millions of years, so the "discovery" was bound to create considerable excitement. I was called in as the local zoological expert to give my views.

Terence Coffin-Grey, the museum's technical officer, joined in the joke and produced a most realistic looking pterodactyl, skillfully attaching the head and neck of a hornbill to the body of a huge fruit bat. On the head of the hornbill a serrated comb-like structure was fixed and a "third eye" was set in the head. The "monster" was then preserved in a large jar in a weak solution of formalin; with the addition of a mutilated ostrich egg, the pterodactyl was presented to the public.

Between us we fooled thousands of viewers. Telephone inquiries began pouring in, and when I was asked if the discovery really was true, I had to explain that it had been an April-fool hoax.

Next day at the museum I was summoned to the director's office and Roger Summers told me, without mincing words, that I was employed by a scientific institution, and was expected to behave in a more responsible and dignified manner. He said my behavior had been disgraceful, and I was left in no doubt as to what was expected of me.

I tackled my new job with enthusiasm, and thoroughly enjoyed it. A lot of my time was spent answering queries from the public.

One day a lady phoned to ask if snakes could hatch from a clutch of eggs laid by her pet tortoise. I tried to tell her that if eggs laid by a tortoise were fertile, only baby tortoises would hatch from them. She was not convinced, however, and said her gardener had assured her that snakes would hatch from the eggs, and since he had been born in the country, he would surely know.

A farmer appeared at the museum with a pair of kudu horns. One was normal with the typical kudu spiral but the other was deformed, and very closely resembled a sable horn but without ridges at the base. It was merely a deformed horn. The farmer insisted that the horns were from a kudu/sable cross. He had often seen that type of hybrid before, he said. I tried to explain that there was no such thing as a wild kudu/sable hybrid and that the horns were from a kudu. His response to my explanation was, "That's the trouble with you museum people, you think you know everything."

Most visitors were easy to deal with and I took pleasure in helping them. People began to bring in wounded birds and animals hoping I would help heal them. Although acting as a local veterinary surgeon was not part of the job, I was anxious to assist. Whenever I could, I would "repair" a bird and if possible, release it. Many ex-pets were also brought to the museum, and I could not bring myself to putting them down, so many ended up at my home.

I also researched aspects of mammalogy and reproductive physiology, and had papers published in scientific journals throughout the world. I completed a detailed thesis on *Game and Tsetse Flies* for which I was admitted to Membership of the Institute of Biologists in London.

I enjoyed field-work and expeditions the most. I went into the bush on every opportunity and was lucky enough to go on several long expeditions into Botswana, visiting the Kalahari Desert twice, and also the Okavango Swamps.

On one memorable trip into the Kalahari with Dr. Reay Smithers, we were accompanied by Professor Bill Elder, a visiting zoologist from the University of Missouri. We travelled south to Debeeti on the main road, and then turned northward into the desert. The loose sand was often soft and deep, requiring the use of four-wheel drive for miles at a time. We often passed herds of gemsbok and red hartebeest, and from time to time flocks of ostriches.

One evening, crossing a large, open stretch of desert, we ran into a terrifying sandstorm. The wind blew furiously and when it eventually subsided we were covered in fine red dust; a most unpleasant experience.

Technical staff erecting a
skeleton of a giraffe at the
Natural History Museum

Natural History Museum in Bulawayo where the author was at one time Curator of
Mammals and then Director

Shortly after establishing camp north of Lephepe, we encountered a band of Bushmen. This is the oldest race in Botswana. According to some experts, Bushmen have inhabited the country for about 14,000 years. They are hunters and food gatherers, and always have been. They experience the same extreme climatic conditions in the desert as do the plants and animals, and have survived and adapted equally well. Because of centuries of isolation, they are afraid of anything unknown, especially strange people. I found the group we encountered very cautious and wary of us. It took a long time to overcome their shyness before they would accept meat that I offered. In exchange, they gave me a bow and several arrows, a couple of ostrich eggs, a stabbing spear and a musical instrument. All the bartering was done by sign language.

Bushmen are not wasteful hunters. They kill only what they require, and thus they duplicate the role of any other predator in the vast central desert. Their hunting techniques cause little if any disturbance to the balance of game, and with their tiny bows and poison arrows, which have a very short range, they must carefully stalk their prey for success.

Hunting usually takes place in the very early morning or in late afternoon, when it is cool. When an animal is wounded it is never chased, for it will soon succumb to the poison on the arrow. A wounded animal will stop running within minutes of being hit, if it is not followed. The Bushmen, knowing this, make the best of their short hunting excursions. Because of the poor vegetation cover in many parts of the desert, they have to rely on their skill and patience.

Steenbok and duiker form the bulk of the meat eaten by Bushmen. These two little antelope are easily snared and both are common in the desert. Both species are territorial; that is, they frequent the same area for long periods. As a result they usually use the same paths. The Bushmen, knowing their habits, set snares on the paths, and with the aid of barriers of cut branches, sticks and grass, they can direct the antelope into the snares.

Springbok and gemsbok are two other common species of the desert and these are shot with arrows, when they can get close enough. The Bushmen's diet also includes tortoises, rodents, snakes, springhares, porcupines, jackals and birds, as well as ants and termites. The poison used on their arrows is taken from the larvae of the leaf-cutting beetle.

Although hunting is extremely important to them, food-gathering is even more essential. They rely more on plants for food than they do on animals. The collection of food-plants is the main task of the women. A group can go without meat for long periods but it could not survive for more than a few weeks without plants.

114

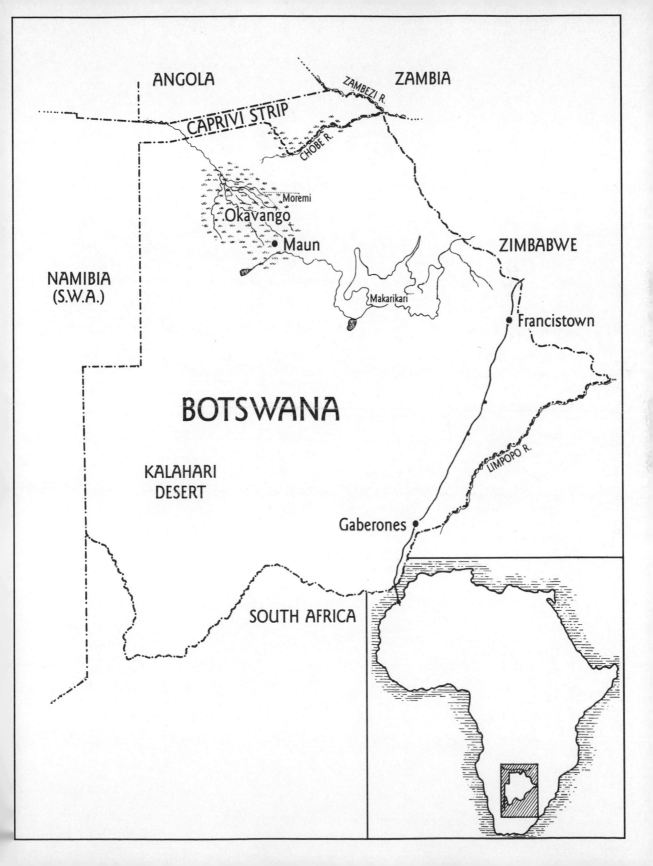

The author when employed in the Research Branch of the Department of National Parks and Wildlife Management, Zimbabwe

The tsamma melon is readily eaten by the Bushmen as well as by many species of game. I have eaten the melons on many occasions and can appreciate why they are so highly prized by the Bushmen. They taste a lot like a watermelon, yet have the flavor of a cucumber, and have extremely high water and vitamin C content. Other plants important to the Bushmen are the various species of donkey-berries which are high in sugar and starch, and are eaten raw; also the pods of the bauhenia tree which have a high food value. Fruits, especially the sour plum, are readily eaten when available.

Over the weeks that we spent in the desert, I found three abandoned Bushmen camps, and in each instance I was amazed at the large number of tortoise shells left lying on the ground. At one camp I found 85 shells scattered around.

The Bushmen make the most of the environment, with maximum efficiency, and extract the greatest possible use of all the resources available to them.

In contrast to the dryness and hardships of the Kalahari Desert, the Okavango Swamps are a veritable Garden of Eden. One thinks of a swamp as an area of dirty, muddy water with a mass of rotting vegetation. Not so the Okavango. Before I visited the Moremi Game Reserve on the eastern side of the Okavango, I pictured a conventional swamp. Instead I found a beautiful lake with patches of marsh and crystal-clear water. The whole area lies in the northern part of the Kalahari Desert, and the swamps are fed by the magnificent Okavango River which has its source in Angola.

When it reaches Botswana it is a broad, single river, but some way downstream it divides and subdivides, broadening out into hundreds of channels, to form the delta of the main swamp.

There are two very large land areas in the swamps: Chief's Island, and the Moremi Wild Life Reserve, which is a large triangle of land. Seasonally moist, grass-covered glades occur throughout the region, and in these there is an abundance of game. The red lechwe is extremely common and late one afternoon I counted 160 feeding together in shallow water. Aquatic grasses with small patches of reeds covered the flooded area.

One day as I was watching a herd of 17 animals feeding on aquatic plants, about 15 feet from dry land, a pack of eight wild dogs suddenly appeared. What a wonderful sight to watch the lechwe racing through the water in a series of plunges, their horns laid flat back against their shoulders. When the water was about two feet deep they stopped. As if they had been given some strange signal, they all turned to face the wild dogs still standing on dry land. The dogs, losing interest, had a quick drink and disappeared into the mopane woodland as mysteriously as they had arrived. The lechwe waited about 20 minutes and then started moving into shallow water again.

116

Lone elephant bull at Guvulala Pan in the Hwange National Park (Zimbabwe)

Orphaned lion cubs "Shashi" and "Shangani" soon after arriving at Chipangali Wildlife Orphanage

A female lion on a kill at Hwange National Park

"Shangani" at three years old, still at Chipangali
Wildlife Orphanage

"Tiki" the cheetah at Chipangali Wildlife Orphanage

Wild-dogs (Cape hunting dogs) in the Luangwa Valley, Zambia

Part of the Victoria Falls, Zimbabwe

A good example of balancing rocks in the Matopos Hills in western Zimbabwe

Giraffe as featured in the rock art in the spectacular granite hills of the Matopos near Bulawayo, Zimbabwe

An adult male klipspringer clearly showing the position of the preorbital (face glands) in front of the eye

The klipspringer has most interesting hooves which enable it to move about with ease on the rocky outcrops on which it lives

The serval is one of the most beautiful small spotted cats found in Africa

A female white or square-lipped rhino with her calf in the Umfolozi Game Reserve in Zululand, South Africa

An adult black rhino in the Luangwa Valley in Zambia. Black rhino have now been poached to near-extinction in this beautiful valley.

One of the female lions at Chipangali with her newly born cub

A "Bushman" male in the Kalahari Desert in Botswana

A "Batonka" lady in the Zambezi Valley in Zimbabwe. It was in this area where the rhino capture operation took place in 1965.

"Mukwa" and "Muchibi," the two orphaned elephants at Chipangali Wildlife Orphanage with "Suzi" the kudu

An immature brown snake eagle

The black-shouldered kite

A dark chanting goshawk

Little banded goshawk

Little sparrow hawk

Immature barn owl

SOME OF THE BIRDS OF PREY BROUGHT TO CHIPANGALI

An adult male caracal (lynx) can be a very vicious predator and a most skillful hunter of hares and game birds

One of the caracal kittens born in captivity at Chipangali Wildlife Orphanage

In captivity caracals often have two or more kittens. This pair was born at Chipangali.

"Ingwe" the leopard at about three weeks old

Even when over two years old, "Ingwe" could still be taken out into the wild near Chipangali Wildlife Orphanage

The blue duiker of southern Africa

The bay duiker of central and west Africa

The most common of all duiker in Africa — the crowned or bush duiker

The zebra or banded duiker of Liberia, Sierra Leone and the Ivory Coast

SOME OF THE VERY MANY SPECIES OF DUIKER TO BE FOUND IN AFRICA

The continental ice shelf of Antarctica with the "RSA"

For many days we sailed through the very rough seas of the South Atlantic in order to reach Antarctica

The last remaining pieces of what was once an iceberg

The Antarctic Ice Shelf near Muskeg Bukta in Antarctica

Natives in dugout canoe — Okavango Swamps, Botswana

Another fantastic swamp antelope is the sitatunga. The first wild sitatunga I saw was in the Moremi area. I was spellbound when a group of five stood watching me early one morning. They were in about two feet of water, in a cluster of papyrus and phragmites reeds, and made no effort to run and hide. There were four females and a single large male. The females were beautiful beyond words, their bright-red coats standing out clearly against the background of green reeds. The female is much more beautiful than the male, with distinct white lateral bands, and white spots on the haunches. The male was very much larger, and in addition to a magnificent pair of horns, was much darker than the females.

The reedbuck also spends a great deal of time on the flood plain. It will venture into water when disturbed, but generally it occurs on the margins of the great flood plains in the Kwaai area, and is plentiful in some parts of the Moremi Wild Life Reserve.

The bird life of the Okavango provides a glimpse of paradise. Vast flocks of ducks of many species abound, especially red-billed teal and white-faced duck. What I loved more than any other was the beautiful dwarf-goose. Almost every stretch of water with lilies and other aquatic plants supported small flocks of these geese. Nowhere in Africa had I seen such concentrations of duck as lived in the swamps. Crested cranes, saddle-billed storks, and dozens of species of other water birds abounded throughout the area.

When the Okavango River comes down in flood, about March and April, the streams overflow and the dry flood plains soak up the water. The water spreads in all directions and as a result all manner of insects and reptiles are flushed out of their hiding places. The insect refugees and small mammals, also made homeless, attract the birds, and I often saw hundreds of crested cranes and saddle-billed storks feeding at the water's edge.

Lion, leopard and cheetah and many of the smaller carnivores are common in this entire delta.

The Moremi Wild Life Reserve, indeed the whole Okavango area, is a wonderful and beautiful part of Africa, and I pray it stays unspoiled and undeveloped.

CHAPTER FOURTEEN

A DREAM COME TRUE

IN AUGUST 1969, as the museum mammalogist, I was assigned to make a detailed survey of Zimbabwe's largest wildlife sanctuary, Hwange National Park. The survey lasted two years and I made six major field expeditions, and innumerable shorter visits there.

I was to produce a complete list of the park's mammals, to study the habits and observe the smaller carnivores and nocturnal animals. This meant going out at night and spending hundreds of hours behind a dazzling light in an open Land-Rover. It was a most rewarding and stimulating experience, especially when elephant were about. It was also terrifying at times.

Late one afternoon as I was driving slowly on the large, open area below Sinamatella Camp, I spotted dozens of vultures sitting in trees close to a dry riverbed. As I approached, many took off and settled in trees a short distance away. I looked for a carcass; there had to be one with so many vultures gathered.

Sure enough, there it was. A large dead elephant lay in the riverbed, about 50 yards away. I wondered why no vultures were sitting on the body, so I stopped the vehicle, got out, and looked down from the high bank. Puzzled by the situation, I jumped down the nine-foot bank. At the carcass I could see no reason for the vultures' reluctance to feed.

Touching the elephant, and walking slowly around it several times, I suddenly got the fright of my life. A thundering, hair-raising lion's roar pierced the stillness of the bush. From not 10 yards away, under a cluster of acacia bushes, a large lion emerged. Without a split second's thought I sprinted across the soft sand, took one mighty leap up the bank and dived into the Land-Rover. I was a champion runner at my school, but

I never covered the ground as quickly as I did that day. I sat for a few minutes to recover my wits and take stock of the situation.

The lion returned to his hiding place. He apparently did not intend to harm me, for he easily could have caught me before I reached the bank if he had wanted to. I sat for half-an-hour, watching to see if anything would happen. Nothing did, and it was getting dark. I drove back to camp, a more alert and wiser man.

Next day I returned to the carcass, this time with much more caution. I could see that the elephant's body had been opened and a lot of meat eaten. Hundreds more vultures had gathered — the place was literally alive with them. They were sitting on the sand and on the bank, but still well away from the carcass. As I sat quietly watching, two great lappet-faced vultures peeled out of the sky and settled close to the elephant. One stood for a few seconds before moving. The other bounced along with spread wings to the open part of the elephant. Just as he was about to poke his head into the huge hole, two lions stormed out of the bushes and nearly caught him. I have never seen a vulture with such agility. It took off almost vertically, and was instantly out of reach of the great cats.

Fascinated, I moved my Land-Rover into the shade of a tree, and sat there for two hours, watching the pantomime. Each time a vulture appeared on the carcass, one or both lions would rush out and drive it away.

Three days later the two old lions were still there and the vultures were in the trees. I had to move on, so I never did see if the vultures finally got a share of the decaying meat.

On another occasion it was an elephant that gave me some anxious minutes. Two senior wardens and I were cruising along a rough bush-track in the park. A game scout and an Alsatian dog were in the back.

Unexpectedly we came face to face with a herd of elephant, mostly cows and calves. We stopped for a few minutes as they crossed the road ahead of us. All of a sudden, without provocation, one old cow decided to charge. She opened her ears, rolled up her trunk, started screaming, and stormed down at us. We remained dead still, and she stopped about 15 yards from the Land-Rover. She stood there for a few minutes, then walked away. A few minutes later she repeated her charge, and this time her attack was aimed more to the left side of the vehicle, where I was sitting by the open door. She came on and on, stopping only 10 yards away.

By this time I was feeling rather uneasy in my exposed position. The African in the back of the open vehicle looked pale with fright. The cow turned again and moved away, and as she did so, her tummy rumbled nervously. So did mine! Once more she swung

Elephant at water hole in Hwange National Park, Zimbabwe

around and charged, stopping five feet away from me this time. I could feel her breathing over me, and I found myself pushing hard against my neighbor in the middle seat. The driver found the whole episode rather amusing, since he was well out of harm's way, on the opposite side.

In my nervous state I visualized the mammoth, infuriated elephant pushing her long, white tusks through me, or turning over the Land-Rover. As she moved away again, I insisted that we leave immediately. I was not prepared for another look at the trunk and tusks at such close quarters. We drove off along the bush-track, the cow following us for some distance, screaming and ears flapping. I was relieved to see the last of her.

Elephant during the day are not really a problem, but at night, and especially with a petrified driver, it's another matter. During the survey Tobias, the museum driver, accompanied me on the various expeditions. He was truly afraid of elephants. If he spotted one at night, he would drive off at great speed, with no consideration for his passengers. We would have to abandon our spotlight and hold on for dear life to avoid being thrown from the vehicle. Seeing an elephant at night always had the same effect on Tobias.

I enjoyed the mammal survey work at Hwange, and loved every second out in the bush, whether counting game at night or sitting at a pan observing the different animals.

––––––––––

In 1972 I was appointed Director of the Natural History Museum, but continued as mammalogist as well. I had reached the top of the museum tree in Bulawayo and recalled with some amusement having been refused a more lowly post many years previously.

As time passed I became more and more disenchanted with administration, board meetings and having to "act the part" of director. I was known as the "casual director" for I refused to conform to "collar-and-tie" standards, preferring my open-neck shirts and shorts.

By this time my collection of orphaned, sick and abandoned animals had grown to a very large family. I had about 50 and the property I owned outside Bulawayo became too small. In 1972 I married Patricia Ann (Paddy) who helped a great deal with the animals. We bought a 100-acre farm at Worringham, 15 miles from the city, with a beautiful view of the Matopo Hills. We loved the place at once, and since I had spent so many happy years in the Chipangali area in Eastern Zambia, we named

Animals at pan (water hole) in the Hwange National Park

our own refuge "Chipangali." Thus was Chipangali Wildlife Orphanage born in May 1973 — another dream come true.

Paddy, a commercial and wildlife artist, helped with the layout of the cages and gardens, and Chipangali developed most attractively. She prepared all the building plans. When we moved to Chipangali we had a cheetah, two servals, many duiker, a sable, several jackals, a pair of bat-eared foxes, a honey badger, steenbok, monkeys and baboons, dassies and several other animals, and hundreds of birds. Cages and enclosures had to be built for them all. While these were being made Paddy and I camped in a tent under a large fig tree for six weeks.

When the cages and enclosures were finished we built an office and a large nursery-cum-animal-hospital, storeroom, bathroom and feedroom. When it was completed we moved in and started work on our own house. By this time we had spent over $20,000 on Chipangali (excluding the cost of the land). Every cent I had, including what I was given for loss of my job in Zambia, was spent on Chipangali. We still needed money for our own house, so I sold two properties I owned in South Africa. We felt it was all worthwhile when we saw Chipangali begin to become something really useful and important.

It became obvious we would have to admit visitors to our orphanage. At first only a few friends were invited, but we also found that strangers arrived at all hours of the day and night, asking to see the animals. We were delighted by their interest, but the frequent interruptions became a little irritating. We felt that if people wanted to see the animals they should help pay the cost of feeding them, so we put a donation box in a conspicuous place. This did not work. In a group of four or five adults, only one would contribute 10 or 20 cents, and the others nothing. The average donation was less than five cents per person. If we had charged an entrance fee, the same people would quite willingly have paid 50 cents or more to see the animals.

About this time, a small zoo and snake park opened on the Matopos Road several miles from Bulawayo. The owner first came to Chipangali and saw about 50 visitors. He decided to establish a place of his own. I warned him that if he thought he would make money he would be disappointed. However, he went ahead building cages, enclosures, snake pits and duck ponds, and must have spent several thousand dollars. He had a Grand Opening and people flocked to see the place. As the weeks passed, attendance dropped and soon hardly anyone was visiting it. He advertised to buy animals and birds from the public, and his collection multiplied, but there were still few visitors. Eventually it closed and he offered the animals and snakes for sale.

A lady bought two young baboons for $10 each, but after a couple of weeks she realized they were not suitable as pets and asked if we would buy them from her

White rhino in Hwange National Park

Roan antelope at
pan in Hwange
National Park,
Zimbabwe

Lion on a zebra kill in Hwange National Park

for the price she had paid. We have a strict policy at Chipangali never to purchase animals. In fact we insist that people pay us to take them. We told the lady that if she paid us $10 for each baboon we would take them and give them a home. This she did willingly, for she obviously was fond of the animals.

Paddy and I decided reluctantly to open Chipangali to the public, and charge an entrance fee. Toward the middle of 1974, we built a little tea kiosk on our former campsite. We finished a special hothouse for Paddy, built many aviaries for the birds and ducks, and opened to the public on September 12. There were a few visitors, but instead of the usual daily donation total of only four or five dollars, we took in much more; the fee was 35 cents for adults and 25 cents for children. As time went on the number of visitors increased.

One day I was interviewed on TV, and I described Chipangali in detail. Next day (a Sunday) we were inundated — more than 500 people visited throughout the day. On Monday (also a holiday) we had another 600. I had provided a small parking area for about 20 cars, but at one time there were about 200 stacked along the roadway and in the bush.

For weeks Paddy and I had discussed my leaving the National Museum and running Chipangali full time. The number of animals had increased tremendously, and so had the problems. The orphanage required my full attention.

I had considered resigning from time to time but something new always prevented it. Now I made up my mind I would leave as soon as I had finished my publication *Mammals of Wankie National Park*.

Then something wonderful happened which changed my plans again. I attended a lecture on the Antarctic by an old friend, Anthony Hall-Martin, a biologist who had made the first seal survey for the MRI (Mammal Research Institute) at Pretoria University. He told me the MRI planned to send another biologist to the Antarctic to do a second seal study. I applied for this post and to my great delight was accepted. I would sail from Cape Town for the Antarctic in January 1975 with the permission of my museum's trustees.

CHAPTER FIFTEEN

ANTARCTICA

THE "RSA," a tough little round-bottomed ship specially adapted for work in the Antarctic, steamed out of Cape Town on January 10, 1975. With the decks vibrating under me, I felt I was in a world of make-believe, sailing into the magic places I had dreamed about for 30 years. Until Captain James Cook had braved the unknown two centuries before, Antarctica lay undiscovered for 50 million years. The Americans, John Davis and Wilkes Scott, and Amundsen and Shackleton were among the heroic polar explorers who gradually brought a new ocean and a new continent into man's understanding. Now I was off to see, to photograph, and to record this lost frozen world of icebergs, penguins, whales and seals.

My joy was short-lived. The RSA, as I noted, had a round bottom. And no keel. And no stabilizer. She began to roll horribly as soon as we left the harbor and I rushed below, violently ill. That was the start of a miserable couple of days. We were in the sea called the Cape of Storms, so named by early navigators. It certainly lived up to its name. Also, the seamen had told me that RSA stood for "Rolls Slowly Along." My cabin mate, the doctor, gave me an injection and some pills and I felt better.

Alas, that night we struck strong winds and rough seas and the little ship bounced about like a cork. I checked the RSA's roll and could not help thinking that she had been wrongly loaded. She rolled 40 degrees to starboard, making me wonder if she was going right on over, but then rolled only 10 degrees on the port side. Night and day brought the same interminable rolling and tilting and always slowly, oh, so slowly.

We heaved and pitched through the Roaring Forties for two days, averaging only about eight knots, and sailing some 200 miles a day. Antarctica lay 2,000 miles south of Cape Town. Forlornly, I wondered if we would ever get there. The skipper, Captain Ed Funk, said life would improve when we reached Bouvet Island, and he was right.

We had been at sea a week when we sailed into calmer waters. The temperature dropped to 2 °C and the sea to zero, but because of the salt the sea only freezes at several degrees below zero. It was bitterly cold on deck, but what a relief the peace and calm were after the storms we had endured.

We saw our first large iceberg on January 16, which set the cameras clicking away — so much so that the captain had to remind us we would see many more in the days ahead. Indeed, we would see hundreds of icebergs of all colors, shapes and sizes. We passed herds of the giant blue whales which can grow to 90 feet long and weigh up to 100 tons. And sea birds by the thousands. The farther south we sailed the calmer the sea became, and our speed climbed to 10 knots.

When we crossed the Antarctic Circle, there was a wild, hilarious party and a lot of beer was consumed to celebrate the occasion. I am a teetotaler, but I was persuaded to demonstrate a Zulu War Dance at 1:00 A.M., in my underpants, which were not the best protection when the portholes were opened to throw out empty beer cans. In came streams of frozen air. Temperatures were down to near zero.

Next day we passed 60 icebergs in a calm clear sea with absolutely no wind. It was a strange, peaceful atmosphere and though there was no feeling of loneliness, each one of us felt we had been alone that day. It was an unusual and wonderful sensation.

There were now much fewer birds. We passed one iceberg that was strangely bright, sort of an electric blue. It was at least half a mile long with a pinnacle rising about 200 feet at one end.

Here are some extracts from my diary:

Monday, 20 January 1975
The sea was wonderfully calm from the moment I was on deck. Everyone was watching for pack ice, which the captain felt sure we would come into during the day. We saw four herds of killer whales and seven herds of Minke whales, all close to the ship. Several herds had up to seven or eight animals in them. The average seemed to be about four. They rolled in and out of the water, like oversized dolphins, almost gambolling. Just after 11:00 A.M., we saw in the distance a vast wall of ice. We were all certain it was the Antarctica continental ice shelf, but it turned out to be a gigantic iceberg about 15 miles long. Away in the distance we could see the white pack ice; there were more than 30 excited young men on deck, yet the whole place was deathly quiet.

We entered pack ice at 12:30 P.M. How fantastic! It's hard to believe we were on our own planet. I cannot find words to describe the surrounding spectacle — it all seemed so unreal. The eerie

"R.S.A." leaving Cape Town for Antarctica

Iceberg in South Atlantic

beauty of the large blobs of ice and vast flat sheets of broken pack ice are unforgettable. Every now and then the sun's rays shone through some chunk of ice and it appeared blue — not a dark blue, but a magnificent intense light blue.

As we glided through the pack ice I saw about 50 single crab-eater seals, three leopard seals and two Ross seals, all lying on ice floes. They made no effort to leave the ice as we steamed toward or beside them. From time to time we broke through large ice floes where seals were resting, and they were tilted off the ice, sliding into the water. The leopard seals looked quite reptilian and as we approached, one of them sliddered along slowly and opened its mouth wide at us.

We passed thousands of penguins today. The great and beautiful emperor penguin and the small Adelie penguin are found in these parts. They were much more nervous than the seals had been, and when the ship approached an ice floe where they were standing, they dived into the water.

All the penguins near the edge of the ice sheet, in the pack ice or in the water, were either living in the ocean or getting their sustenance from it. Besides the flightless penguins, South Pole skua and the Antarctic petrel are found here. In the Antarctic, and as well as on the sub-Antarctic islands, are terns, albatrosses, cormorants, gulls and several other species. Some birds at times even penetrate onto the continental ice shelf and the interior.

Five of the world's 17 species of penguins are found in this area where we were surveying the seals. The little Adelie averages about 15 inches high, while the big dignified emperor penguin weighs from 60 to 100 pounds, and stands nearly four feet high.

The arctic tern is a most extraordinary bird. It spends about six months a year in the Antarctic and then flies north to spend the rest of the year in the Arctic. It flies more than 11,000 miles a year and lives in almost perpetual daylight.

Astronauts observing Earth from space say that one of the most distinctive features of our planet is the vast ice sheet of Antarctica. It covers 5,500,000 square miles — an area larger than the United States. The ice shelf on the average is about 6,500 feet thick and contains over 90 percent of the world's ice. Only about five percent of the land area of Antarctica is visible above the ice. If the Antarctic melted it would raise the level of the world's oceans by about 150 feet, and flood every seaport and low coastline in the world, including such metropolitan cities as New York, Boston, San Francisco, London and Tokyo.

The Arctic is mostly ocean, while Antarctica is partly land. This largely accounts for the colder climate of Antarctica, where the coldest temperature ever recorded on earth was −88°C.

132

"R.S.A." in pack ice en route to Antarctica

We reached the Antarctic ice shelf on 21 January 1975, and spent the whole day going from one *bukta* (bay) to the next, trying to find the best place to offload the cargo for SANAE (South African National Antarctic Expedition), especially our muskeg vehicles. The first four buktas were all too dangerous. There were crevasses or "lean overs" on the ice shelf, and the sea was much too choppy next to it. Enormous pieces of the shelf were continually breaking off and falling into the sea.

On one occasion I filmed a piece of ice about 200 feet long and 50 feet wide breaking off and falling into the water. The shelf must have been 150 feet high. Fortunately the ship was a good 600 yards from the fall; otherwise it could have been disastrous.

Eventually we found a safe place where the ship could move against the ice shelf and we began offloading everything that was needed for the base. We worked all day in the bright light and freezing weather. By evening my face was painful and red. I had the worst sunburn I had experienced in many years. Our polarized sunglasses provided relief from the sun and we could not have managed without them. Daytime temperature was about −5 °C but with all the heavy work offloading cargo, I was very hot. We all sweated heavily from the work in spite of the freezing cold. One only realized the extent of the cold when gloves came off.

It was still daylight at 7:00 P.M., and we discovered that the ice shelf where we were moored had a very large cavity just at sea level about 10 feet high and nine feet deep. This was of course very dangerous and we had to stop offloading at once, and put to sea. In my diary I wrote, "God alone knows when it will be suitable to complete the offloading task."

I need not have worried. Herr Funk, the captain, rammed the ice shelf about 15 times with the bow of the ship to loosen soft ice. Each time vast chunks, some weighing many tons, would be sliced off and come crashing into the water. We were able to dock again at 11:00 P.M.

Friday, January 24, 1975

Early this morning we set out over land to the SANAE base on a muskeg vehicle, the 11 miles taking us about 90 minutes. The ice, although hard, was very bumpy. The prevailing wind makes long ridges across the otherwise flat surface. We could see for miles. By the time we reached base the sky was clear and it was bitterly cold. The air temperature had dropped to −11 °C, the coldest since our arrival. We spent a few hours underground, or rather "under ice," at the base.

The original buildings were once on the surface but as ice and snow piled up each year, they became covered. Eventually entrance to the buildings was made through a hole in the roof. The entire building is 50 feet below the surface.

The base could have been a lot cleaner than it was. The ice passages as they are called (the walls consist of dripping ice and the floors are also ice) were full of empty tins and boxes. The

134

Weddel seal on pack ice

Antarctic ice shelf

little kitchen was dirty and smelly and the entire living room area reeked. The stink of cigarette and pipe smoke filled the whole place.

Pictures of nude women covered every inch of the walls, the beams on the ceiling and the ceiling as well. There was every conceivable type of picture, including a series of 15 that would have spelled trouble for the owners almost anywhere else in the world. The radio room, laboratory and sleeping quarters all displayed the same "artistic" taste.

After spending a few hours at the base we loaded a sled with a tent and food, hitched up eight huskies and set off directly southward into the ice. At 7:00 P.M. we pitched our tent and made a meal of tinned meat, mixed vegetables and stewed dried fruit, followed by coffee. The dogs were given a special protein mixture. They can manage about 18 miles a day.

It was bitterly cold with the temperature down to −17°C. I decided then and there that I hated that cold. My cameras all froze up in spite of wrapping them in blankets. I was wearing my short underpants, long underpants, a string vest, a woolen vest, a shirt, two jerseys, a green anorak, jeans and anorak trousers, a Balaclava (from Bulawayo) over my head and ears and an Arctic sheepskin hat, and in spite of also wrapping myself in my blanket, I was still cold.

At last the day ended when the sun set at 12:05 A.M. Ten minutes later it was up again, seemingly only a few feet away from where it had gone down. One has to see it to believe it!

None of us slept well and we were out of our sleeping bags and the tent by 8:00 A.M., in spite of the temptation to stay there all day. My skin felt like dry parchment. A little snow had fallen during the night and the dogs, which were tied up outside, were covered. They were curled up for warmth with their noses buried in their bellies. They did not move until we emerged from our tent, whereupon they yelped and jumped about with joy. It amazed me to see how they slept out in the open in that weather.

We cheered ourselves up with a hot meal and moved on southward. There was nothing but snow and ice. No living thing could be seen in this colorless, featureless white waste. I kept wondering how it was that men would deliberately challenge such forbidding places that brought them such hardship and danger.

By 11:00 A.M., the temperature read −21°C. My very breath froze on my beard and moustache and I was grateful I had grown such good protection for my face. It was now too cold to go on, so we pitched our tent and crawled into our beds. The bitter wind blew so fiercely that twice we had to get out and peg down the flapping tent.

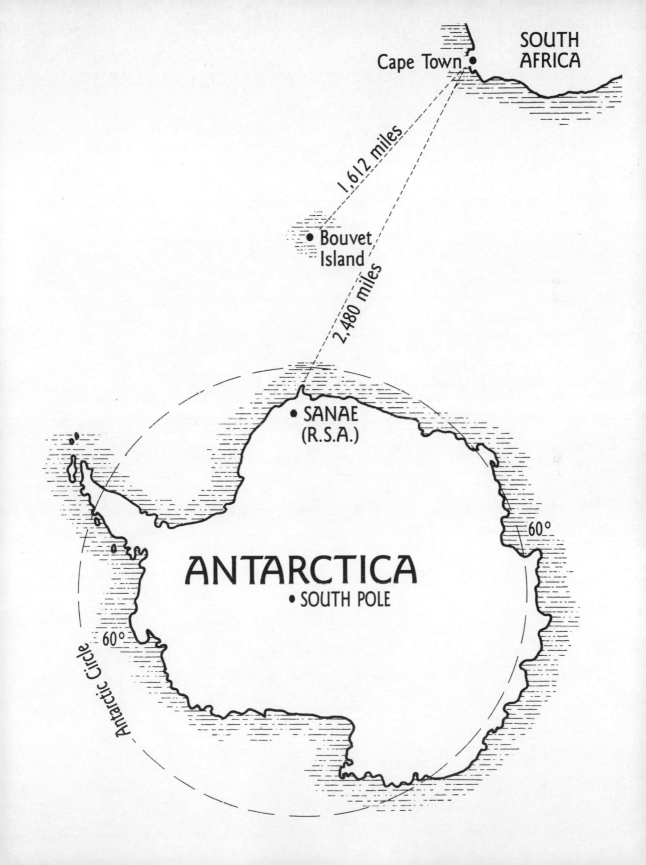

SOUTH
AFRICA

Cape Town

1,612 miles

• Bouvet
Island

2,480 miles

• SANAE
(R.S.A.)

ANTARCTICA

• SOUTH POLE

60°

60°

Antarctic Circle

At 10:00 P.M., it was still quite light outside but the wind had dropped and it was relatively warm again (only −11°C) and quite pleasant! We were glad to return to base, and back at the ship I set about in earnest on my main reason for being there — to make a survey of the seals in the pack ice surrounding the ice shelf. (Later back in Bulawayo I published the results in the *South African Journal of Antarctic Research*.)

January 30th was a frightening day. On our return to our regular mooring, which had been free the day before, we found that wind and tide had pushed heavy pack ice hard up against the ice shelf where we normally moored. To make a bad position worse, a large iceberg was jammed against the shelf near our entrance to Muskeg Bukta. And worse yet, as we were maneuvering through the ice pack past the stranded iceberg, another enormous floating hill of ice, about 80 feet high and half a mile long, began to drift toward us at one or two knots an hour. Meanwhile we were trying to butt our way through very dense ice at slow speed.

We were in danger of being crushed between the two gigantic ice masses. Just in time the captain realized we would never get through the rapidly narrowing gap, and ice pack pressure on the vessel was building up by the second. He quickly put the ship in reverse. For a sickening moment it seemed we would never make it. Then very, very slowly the RSA began to move backward. As we did so the ice promptly closed into the gap we left ahead of the bow. Gradually we drew away from the danger. Everyone on board gave sighs of relief.

We were about a mile away when the two great icebergs collided. In spite of the distance we could clearly hear the tons of pack ice crumbling like a wad of paper. We watched in awe from the deck, thinking what might have been had we been trapped there. Each of us felt so insignificant, so very small in that vast white world.

The captain decided that since the pack ice would block the bay for many days, there was no point in trying to get back. Instead, we set about our next task, that of measuring the rate of continental drift. Africa and Antarctica have been moving apart at about an inch a year for eons. By studying patterns of magnetism on relatively new rocks on the ocean bed, scientists feel they can measure the rate of this drift.

Seventy years ago Alfred Wegener, a North Pole explorer, put forward the theory that all the continents had once been locked together in one great land mass, and that gradually they had drifted apart. The last to break away, he postulated, was the southern block which he called "Gondwanaland." Then fossil rocks found with the remains of Scott's ill-fated expedition, led a British scientist to suggest that they were similar to fossil material in South Africa and Australia.

Our voyage toward the mid-Atlantic would take about 14 days. The scientists on board would measure the magnetization of the rocks on the ocean bed and carry out a number of other projects. Meanwhile I would record and study seals, whales and sea birds during the journey.

We sailed northward, passed through the vast ring of pack ice surrounding Antarctica, and headed for the open sea. On February 4th the barometer showed an abnormally low pressure, indicating that a storm was brewing. That day I managed to get through to Paddy by radio telephone. It was wonderful to be able to speak to her, although the reception was so bad we could hardly hear each other. But I was so glad to be able to tell her how much I loved her. Of course I did not mention the possibility of a big storm ahead of us.

My life in the bush, forests and deserts of Africa had brought me many dangers and discomforts. I had slept in the cold and rain, been swept down swollen, flooded rivers and had many narrow escapes from lions, leopards, elephants, rhinos and black mambas. These were very frightening in their way at the time, but none left the lasting impression that that storm did. Until then I had never really been afraid.

A terrible wind and rough seas suddenly struck our tiny ship. That night waves of 25 to 30 feet were rolling past us. The continuous wind was Force Six to Seven (25 to 30 miles an hour).

From my cabin porthole I saw huge waves rising above the ship, and when they broke over the bow, there was flooding everywhere. I felt really ill, not from seasickness, but from the shock of the situation.

I slept little if at all, and next day the storm got worse. By afternoon the waves were more than 40 feet high. The wind speed was over 50 miles an hour and I feared our tiny ship could not survive. My thoughts turned to the unsinkable "Titanic," which did not help. By the sixth day out, the worst had just begun. The captain instructed us in a fire drill, and in the use of the lifeboats. We were again shown how to lower the boats and we knew this meant even the captain was worried. February 6th was Paddy's birthday and I thought of her often.

Meanwhile the ship was steering straight into the storm, apparently the wisest thing to do. At about 9:00 P.M., Don Main, the chief officer, told Captain Funk they could no longer keep the ship into the wind. She was now blowing slightly sideways. The captain immediately decided we had to change course and go with the wind.

It was not quite as easy as that. The wind was now raging at 70 miles an hour. The waves were 50 feet high. The ship's bridge was only 30 feet above the water

Author Viv Wilson with husky in Antarctica

line, so the waves were well above us. The captain knew that when we turned, it had to be done as quickly as possible.

As the ship wheeled port side, the wind and waves caught us, and for a moment I was certain we would overturn and sink. The waves broke right over us and water poured in from the starboard side. Captain Funk never showed the slightest sign of anxiety and slowly the ship swung around until we were in line, with the storm's wind behind us.

While we steered into the storm, our speed was 1½ to 2 knots an hour, tilting and rolling with each huge swell as we tried to sail up the sides of the waves. Now with the wind behind us we were moving at about 12 to 14 knots an hour and heading straight back toward Antarctica. In deafening roars, vast waves were crashing over the ship. We were many miles off course but could do nothing about it.

For days no work was done on the ship. People kept very much to themselves and there was little conversation. Our inner thoughts were our own secrets. The dreadful storm lasted until February 9th. I had not eaten for several days and lost about 20 pounds. I saw little of the others on the ship. Later I learned that my shipmates had been just as shocked by the experience as I was.

On February 10th the storm subsided and for the first time in six days things began to return to normal. The sea began to calm and the wind dropped. There were still high waves about but the storm was over. Slowly we headed back to the Antarctic continent, now many miles away, and I was able to get back to my work on seals, birds and whales. I caught several Adelie and emperor penguins, and shot a few seals as part of the survey. At last, toward the end of February, we started back to Cape Town.

On the way home we passed what has to be the most isolated piece of land on earth. Bouvet Island, or Bouvetoya to give it its Norwegian name, is about six miles long by four miles wide, and its highest point is 2,000 feet above sea level. There is no other land mass within a 1,000-mile radius.

Normally I hate concrete jungles but what a pleasure it was to see Cape Town again. And to add to my delight, Paddy had flown there to meet me.

Now, at 41, I had fulfilled all three boyhood dreams. I had had exceptional success in each enterprise. The third one, the Antarctic, was the most exhilarating and frightening expedition of my life. Back in Bulawayo I resigned from the museum to build up that new dream which meant so much to me and my family — Chipangali Wildlife Orphanage.

CHAPTER SIXTEEN

CHEEKY, THE HONEY BADGER

I COULD HEAR the phone ringing crisply and loudly in the National Museum in Bulawayo, and wondered if I should leave my work to answer it. My eyes were "weepy" from the formalin fumes, and drops of formalin had even found their way into my surgical gloves and the animal scratches on my fingers. It was a relief to leave the "spirit room." I took off my gloves and rubbed my eyes as I passed cabinets of study-specimens on my way to the telephone. The call came from an old friend, Dave Blake. "Hello, Viv," he said. "Would you like a young, tame honey badger?"

My reaction was one of incredulous excitement, and without hesitation I said, "You're joking!" But the offer was real enough and off I went to Harare to collect the animal. Honey badgers have the reputation of being aggressive and dangerous, and quite capable of killing prey many times their size, so I was a little nervous about my new orphan, and had reservations about giving him a home. But my fears were unfounded. He turned out to be one of the finest animals I've ever owned.

"Midrid," as he was called, was found by an African herdsman when he was only a couple of weeks old. His eyes were open but he was very small and unsteady on his legs, partly from hunger and weakness. He had several long raw scratches on his belly and was in poor condition. He had been found in long grass several hundred yards from a river, and the farmer who had cared for him said there was no sign of a nest or hiding place. The mother was nowhere to be found; the cub was obviously lost or abandoned.

Mrs. Milbank, the farmer's wife, reared Midrid, feeding him cow's milk and glucose from an eyedropper. With constant attention and loving care the little orphan flourished.

141

Midrid was never confined to a cage, having the free run of the Milbank house. He loved climbing over the furniture, and he became more and more independent as he matured. When he was 6½ months old, he attacked and almost killed the Milbanks' Pekingese. Whenever scolded, he would roll over on his back and suck his toes as if saying, "Sorry, I didn't mean to be naughty."

When Midrid insisted on getting into bed and sleeping with the Milbanks' small son, they decided they had to find a home for him. He was 7½ months old when I collected him. At first he snarled at me and kept biting the wire of his cage in an attempt to free himself. He looked extremely unhappy. Because of his "cheekiness," we changed his name to Cheeky.

I took him to Bulawayo, hundreds of miles from where he had been born, and kept him in a cage. He was powerful and quite capable of biting holes in any normal fence with his short, strong, blunt teeth, so we had to build a special cage. Some cornmeal sacks in a 20 gallon drum provided Cheeky his sleeping den. He loved to hide under the sacks after he had rolled them and himself into a ball.

I hated to see him pace up and down in his cage, continually seeking attention, so I took him out as often as possible for walks, or runs, around the yard. He often entered the house, but caused such havoc that we put it "off limits." Kevin and Barry loved Cheeky more than any other of our animals; he was also Paddy's favorite, but because he was often very rough with her, she became nervous around him as he got older.

When we moved to Chipangali, Cheeky was the first to transfer. He loved his new home, for he was allowed out of his cage a lot more than before. Barry took him to the river where they played in the water. Barry spent hours catching crabs, frogs and fish, and Cheeky thoroughly enjoyed the expeditions. He joined in the fun catching his own crabs. He would bite them three or four times, and then feed on them, but Barry needed them alive for his aquarium. When a crab was spotted there was often a scramble and a lot of splashing as each tried to get the prize. Both Barry and Cheeky usually returned home wet and muddy.

One day when Cheeky had been with us more than a year he went to the river with Barry and another youth. On the way he stuck his nose into every hole he could find searching for food. By then he was quite capable of killing snakes, birds and other wild creatures, and wrought havoc decimating my ducks and poultry. We never punished him because he was only acting instinctively. Once he caught a monstrous crab with very large claws. It grabbed him by the nose and he flicked his head sideways, throwing it into the air. As it landed he pounced on it, biting it to pieces.

142

Kevin and Barry with
Cheeky the honey badger

Cheeky, the honey badger, with bat-eared foxes

On this particular day, when he had had enough of the river, the crabs and the children, he climbed onto the river bank and within six yards of where the children were playing he found a termite mound about two feet high. In the side, near the base, was a small hole about three inches in diameter. Cheeky demolished the area with his powerful front feet, and when the hole was large enough, he stuck his head in. Suddenly he yelped loudly and jumped back, rubbing his face on the ground and in the grass. Barry thought he might have been nipped by one of the large termites, as many were crawling about after their mound was opened. A few seconds later Cheeky returned to the hole and was about to attack something inside when Barry grabbed him by the loose skin on his neck and pulled him away. In the bottom of the hole was a cobra. Barry could not tell if it was an Egyptian or a blacknecked spitting cobra. Both are common in the Chipangali area and I had warned the children never to get too close to them, and to call me immediately if they saw one.

Cheeky continued rubbing his eyes and face on the ground and Barry noticed that his eyes were very swollen and nearly closed. Barry was only seven at the time and he covered the half mile up the hill to Chipangali in record time, yelling for me at the top of his voice, "Daddy, Daddy, come quickly! Cheeky has been bitten by a snake." I sprinted down the hill and found Cheeky rolling about, scratching his eyes and crying softly. He was obviously in great pain.

I had to get Cheeky to the house at once, but did not want the snake to escape. Covering my eyes with my left hand, I peeped between my fingers into the hole. A jet of venom splashed against my hand and forehead. At least it was identified! With a large flat stone I closed the entrance to the hole and told Barry's friend to make sure the snake did not escape while I took Cheeky to the house for treatment.

I had hurt my back the week before, so it was a real battle carrying the wriggling 30-pound Cheeky. At the house, he struggled and scratched as we bathed his eyes in a solution of snake-serum and water. Three of us held him down while Paddy washed his eyes, and by the time we finished he was a sorry sight. He was put in his cage and I returned to the river, with a shotgun, and disposed of the snake. Normally I would not kill a snake but with the children spending a lot of time at the river, I was not going to let it get away. I removed the head of the snake and gave the body to Cheeky. Within an hour he was none the worse for his ordeal, and made short work of the snake, devouring it completely. He then coiled himself into a ball under his sack and slept peacefully.

Whenever Cheeky was taken for a walk he found something to eat. He ate crabs, lizards and frogs, and on one occasion he found a francolin's nest and devoured the four eggs in it. No rat was safe if he was about. When he was put into his cage he would run up and down trying to get out, but he was quite different and very happy when he was free — altogether a delightful animal.

Then one day, while his cage was being cleaned, Cheeky escaped, as he had often done before when Paddy or I were there. But on this particular day we were in town. The native workers frightened him as they tried to catch him. The more he ran, the faster the workers ran after him, all yelling *bamba ena, bamba ena* ("catch it, catch it") at the tops of their lungs. He went for miles into the hills, well away from Chipangali.

We spent hours looking for Cheeky. I offered a reward but there was no sign of him. I had often warned the staff at Chipangali not to chase an animal if it got out, and it would eventually return to its home.

One day Cheeky was seen by a friend of mine about a mile from Chipangali. He called "Cheeky, Cheeky" and the animal stopped and stood still for a few minutes, looking at him, and then ambled off into the long grass. He was soon lost in the bushy country. We had three other reports later that he was still alive and had been seen close to Chipangali. But this is broken hilly country, completely wild and uninhabited. Much as I loved Cheeky and wished for his return, I was delighted to know he had survived back in the bush where he was free and happy. It had been a pleasure and privilege to have kept and known such a fine animal, so full of character. He was everything that one could ever have desired in a wild animal. He was also my friend.

———

At Chipangali we have over 70 cages and enclosures with dozens of species of mammals, birds and reptiles, so it is quite understandable that from time to time animals get out. The baboons and monkeys are more often out than in, and what a battle it is to get them back in their cages! There is no possibility of their running away, but it is very inconvenient and annoying spending hours coaxing them back with fruit and delicacies.

Before we cemented their diamond-mesh cage wire into the ground, our two warthogs, "Galoopi" (Daisy) and "Porky" were out almost daily, and much valuable time was spent looking for them in the long grass. Then the tedious business followed of driving them back into the enclosures. Once free they would strut around like miniature rhinos, or run with tail held erect and the tuft of hair on the end flying like a pennant.

Once they were gone for three days. They returned, I believe, because they found life at Chipangali less troublesome, and because they missed their daily meal of grass, fruit and horse-cubes.

One rainy day while I was away in Antarctica, Paddy had a really rough time with the warthogs and one of the monkeys. Togo (the monkey) got out of his cage while the cleaners were working in it, so Paddy sent a group of eight men after him. He was found and isolated in some trees several hundred yards away, but it was impossible to catch him. He kept jumping from one tree to the next. The heavy rain did not help. From time to time Togo jumped onto Paddy's back and then bounced off again into another tree. She was afraid to grab him for he had a fine set of teeth. After two hours she was saturated, and her boots were full of water, so she returned to the house to change, leaving the men to catch the monkey.

When she went outside again she found to her utter disgust, one of the warthogs, Galoopi, running around outside his enclosure. She tried single-handed to get Galoopi back in the pen but could not. Some of the staff attempting to catch Togo were told to drive Galoopi into her enclosure. While they were trying to get Galoopi in, Porky broke out, and both warthogs took off into the long wet grass.

A frustrating hour later Paddy was at her wits' end. She went into the house, sat down, and had a good cry. Half-an-hour later she heard noises. Wiping the tears from her eyes, she went outside, and there were all eight workers coming up the path from the bush. One was carrying Togo, the white-nosed monkey, and the others were herding the warthogs ahead of them. All the animals returned to their enclosures. Paddy went into the house out of the rain and had a much-needed cup of hot tea.

———————

The bush pigs take a perverse delight in giving us as much trouble as possible. Whenever they got loose they would race around the bush and down to the river, knowing that we would soon be after them. They are nasty animals and often become aggressive and even dangerous if chased too hard.

I once received an extremely nasty bite from a large male, "Twighty." He had been free for some hours when we found him in reeds at the riverside. He was chased back into his enclosure and I walked in behind him and closed the gate. Suddenly he swung around, and with arched back and hair raised on his neck and back, he attacked me. I tried to defend myself by slapping him but this annoyed him even more. He grabbed me by the left wrist and bit deeply into my arm, holding on tightly and sinking his teeth into my flesh. He refused to let go, and as he shook his head from side to side, I yelled for help. Six of the staff entered the pen and a real battle followed to get him to release his hold. His jaws had to be forced open. By the time I was eventually freed, my arm was bleeding profusely and was severely bruised. He then attacked anyone near him. He became so uncontrollable and ferocious that

Black-backed jackal at Chipangali Wildlife Orphanage

Adult warthog (foreground) with a young bush pig

I had to shoot him. I was afraid he would break out again and attack the children.

This was the only animal I ever had to destroy at Chipangali because of aggressiveness. He was far more dangerous than any other animal I have owned, and more unpredictable than a leopard. It was a relief to see the last of him. He had killed two of my duiker, and he found great pleasure in chasing Suzie, the female kudu, around the paddock. Although Suzie could jump the six-foot diamond-mesh fence without difficulty, she only did so two or three times. She was so tame she could easily be coaxed back into her enclosure.

Sham, our female impala, could also clear the fence, but she was normally very reluctant to leave the security of the enclosure which she shared with several duiker. The only time she did jump the fence she was so terrified at being outside her "home" that she came bounding over to me, and refused to leave my side. I walked into her enclosure and she followed meekly.

One morning in June 1977, as the staff came on duty, they noticed that the male and female servals had escaped during the night and were standing near the open door of their cage. The male was quickly and quietly driven back, but the female, Janet, the tamer of the two, bolted across some rocks and disappeared into the bush. Paddy and I were away at the time and returned to find Janet missing. The staff, remembering their lesson with Cheeky, knew that under no circumstances should they chase the serval, so they left her in the bush.

We spent many hours looking for her. That night she was seen about half a mile away but she again disappeared for several days. A week later she came into the animal area near the baboon cages but ran off into the bush when we approached her. Then she was seen almost daily during the next week, and each time she moved closer to the staff houses. Finally she was caught in a cage only eight yards from one of the staff rooms. She was thin and scrawny, and I felt so sorry for her. She had only been in the bush for 16 days but was very hungry when captured. She obviously could not survive on her own and needed to be close to humans for food, and possibly companionship. I am convinced that she would have died had she been left in the bush a few days longer.

Servals are not easy animals to release back into the wild. They appear to become more domesticated and accustomed to humans than most other cats. I saw two of these animals die in Zambia when they were returned to the wild, and I also know of one that was killed in the Matopos after being set free. It was a beautiful serval and had been kept as a pet for some time in Harare. Its owner did not want it caged and did not want to give it away. Instead he wanted it freed in the Matopos Park. It was sent to the park's research biologist and caged at the game warden's house

Bat-eared fox at the wildlife orphanage

for several weeks while it was being trained to fend for itself. Some weeks later it was set free. It stayed around the house until it was mauled to death by the watchdog at the camp.

————

Most people regard jackals as distasteful creatures and some will not tolerate them on their land. But the jackal has an important place in nature. It helps clean up carrion, and diseased or injured wildlife in the bush, and without them Africa's wild places would be dirty and diseased. Each year, just before and during the rainy season, young jackals find their way to Chipangali for sanctuary, and I have no hesitation in rearing them for I know I will always be able to return them to the wild.

The young animals are brought to us by police officers, and even farmers who ask us to take and rear them. They are often confiscated from people selling them, and from time to time cubs are found after the mother has been killed.

At Chipangali no attempt is made to tame the young jackals, and they are fed as natural a diet as possible, given dead snakes and other wildlife killed on the roads by automobiles. Dead owls, eagles, hedgehogs, and live frogs and mice are fed to the young who soon learn how to tackle each type of food offered. They are taught to go without food for several days at a time so that when they are eventually released into the wild they do not find the new circumstances too tough.

Jackals are nervous and highly strung carnivores and are always on the run. Even when one watches them in the wild they are usually either running or sleeping. In captivity they are very sensitive. When not sleeping or feeding they are running around their enclosure at a brisk pace, and most people believe they are unhappy. I am convinced this is not so; it is just natural behavior for them to move about a great deal.

————

Not surprisingly, people try out their sense of humor from time to time with telephone hoaxes to Chipangali. I've learned to accept them, and try to be tolerant. So one morning when I had a phone call from a small town named Gwaai, about 150 miles north of Bulawayo, asking if I would like 22 wild-dog puppies, I did not take the call seriously. I said, "Oh yes, I would like 22 wild-dog pups, but I cannot collect them. Please send, or bring them to Chipangali." The caller said "OK, I will." And it was left at that.

I couldn't believe anyone could possibly get 22 wild-dog pups. It is a very rare species and in all the years of collecting orphans, I had never had even one. I thought the whole thing was a joke.

Baby Cape hunting dogs (wild-dogs) — part of the group of 22 orphans brought to Chipangali Orphanage

About three hours later a small pickup truck arrived at Chipangali, and in the back were 22 of the strangest colored puppies I had ever seen, all smelling to high heaven. Talk of wild-dogs to most people in the world, even in Zimbabwe, and most people think you mean domestic dogs that have gone wild. It is necessary to explain that its other name is the Cape hunting dog, and it is a wild Canis just like the dingo in Australia.

When nervous or excited, wild-dog puppies emit a very strong stench. One dog is bad enough so you can imagine what 22 nervous puppies smell like.

In parts of Africa, wild-dogs are notorious livestock killers. But their numbers are dwindling all over the continent and in some African countries they are no longer found.

As far back as the turn of the century, many naturalists regarded wild-dogs as a nuisance. For example, R.C.G. Maughan in a book published in 1914 wrote: "Let us consider for a while that destructive — that blot upon the many interesting wild things — the murderous wild-dog. It will be an excellent day for African game and its preservation when means can be devised for this unnecessary creature's complete extermination."

The day may be close when Africa will lose yet another interesting wild animal as a result of prejudices from people like Maughan, that will spell the end of the species. Recent research shows that the wild-dog is an efficient predator with a highly developed social system. In Zimbabwe, the status of the wild-dog is poor and they are confined mostly to the larger national parks and even in these protected areas, their numbers are now so low that their future is highly endangered.

However, they do kill domestic livestock and this is exactly what happened in the Gwaai area, where the 22 puppies came from. A pack of wild-dogs had killed some cattle belonging to a rancher. He followed the pack and shot several of the adults. Next day, the pups were found at the lair of the mothers who had been shot. Fortunately the rancher was conservation-minded enough to remove the puppies without killing them, and brought them to Chipangali.

The 22 puppies represented four or five litters. Several females will whelp at about the same time, and in the same den, which is what happened in the case of our orphans.

Now came the problem of rearing a large group of pups. We gave eight to friends of ours who agreed to help, and we kept 14 at Chipangali. Over the months six pups died, leaving 16 animals which, as far as we were concerned, was more than enough. The pups grew into beautiful adults. Then they started breeding and I could see problems ahead.

We managed to give two groups of four and another six to ranchers with large properties. We would have preferred to release a whole pack back into the wild if we could have found a suitable area, well away from domestic livestock.

In the meantime, Chipangali still has wild-dogs, and they continue to breed. We are delighted to have such a rare species at the orphanage.

CHAPTER SEVENTEEN

LEOPARDS, LYNXES & LIONS

INGWE, A MALE leopard cub, was born at the Lion and Elephant Motel, not far from the Limpopo River between Zimbabwe and South Africa. The proprietor had had Ingwe's mother since she was a cub and the father had come from Namibia. The pair had produced two previous litters, each of two cubs. When the motel owner decided to dispose of his animals, he gave Ingwe to me.

He was six weeks old when he arrived at Chipangali — a very aggressive and disagreeable animal. He tried to bite and scratch anyone who dared to put hands into his cage. He left his mother only the day before he came to us, and was not really used to humans.

I kept the little chap in a small cage in my office, hoping he would get used to me. I talked to him and tried to touch him whenever I could. At first he objected, but gradually he started eating pieces of meat from my fingers. It took a week before he settled down, and only then did he really take to his meat and milk diet.

Ingwe was let out of his cage several times a day for exercise and to play with Candy, my six-month-old caracal. He was still very nervous and hated strangers or any kind of noise. When I took him for walks, he would run off a short distance and hide, and then scratch and bite when I caught him. My hands and arms were always covered with wounds and plasters.

I tried a collar and lead, hoping that would settle him down, but he hated the restriction and refused to walk if he was so confined. One day I literally dragged him along by the lead until he stopped growling and spitting. He hated every minute, and so did I. I felt cruel and unkind, but the treatment worked wonders. From that day on Ingwe's behavior changed; he seemed to accept the situation and behaved much better. I could even stroke him and play with him.

He grew at a tremendous rate and so did his strength, and when playing with Candy, he was very rough indeed. He often "called" plaintively and I would answer him in a sort of squeak and call his name repeatedly for long periods. We became great friends.

As Ingwe matured, he became more manageable. When I took him for his daily walk he lovingly rubbed himself against me. I was surprised that he became so tame, for at first I was convinced I'd never be able to handle him. His playing became even rougher, however, and he would sometimes leap down on me from the top of a large rock, giving me many bloody wounds.

Kevin and Paddy also suffered from his rough play. One day when Kevin and I took Ingwe to the river for his daily walk, quite unexpectedly he jumped off a large rocky outcrop, straight at Kevin. Just as he sprang, Kevin moved backward. A single claw scraped down Kevin's arm — a three-inch gash that bled profusely. Kevin was shocked and said that in no uncertain terms, he had had enough of Ingwe and would never again go walking with him. I was relieved because I was becoming anxious about Ingwe's roughness, and certainly did not want my child injured.

Paddy had had enough of Ingwe as well. Again it was walk time and Paddy had been assured she would be safe with the leopard. We moved off slowly into the bush, and for some time all went well, with Ingwe bouncing and jumping about in his usual playful manner. It was a pleasure to see him so active. He walked up to Paddy several times, but never close enough to touch her, and she remained cautious. Then he rubbed his head against her and walked around and around her, rubbing his soft silky coat against her legs. She was delighted by his tameness and softness, but a second later Ingwe gave her a hard bite on the ankle. Knowing that he had done wrong, Ingwe shot off into the bush like a streak of lightning.

Paddy yelled with pain and blood flowed freely onto her shoe, covering her foot. She was very upset, and she, too, vowed it was the last time she would walk with us. From then on Ingwe and I had to take our daily walks alone.

Ingwe did just as he pleased, when he pleased, and nothing could change him. He loved playing about in the grass, in the trees and on rocks, his actions the same as a domestic cat. He would try to catch everything that moved, from grasshoppers to leaves blowing in the wind, to even his own flicking tail. His ability to hide and stalk became more expert, and so did his patience. When we first went out he would often stalk and charge me, but as he grew older he took more time, moving patiently and silently, taking up to five minutes before pouncing from a tuft of grass or whatever cover he could find.

A leopard cub is one of the most appealing creatures on earth, and the striking beauty of its eyes is indescribable. Ingwe's eyes changed with his moods. I only had to

Ingwe at four months old

Ingwe at a year old — still tame, very friendly, but very rough

Ingwe relaxing after a long walk

The author with Ingwe — after his daily
free run Ingwe is returned on his lead

Another baby leopard arrives at Chipangali Wildlife Orphanage

Kevin and Barry Wilson with leopard cubs born at Chipangali Wildlife Orphanage

Shangani and Shashi at two months

Shashi and Shangani some months later

look into them to detect his frame of mind. He could see the slightest movement hundreds of yards away, so good was his sight. He often screwed his eyelids into slits, as if to close out the light, when he was unsure of something new and strange. At other times he opened his eyes wide, and just before he charged they would turn a golden-yellow and then, just as suddenly, revert to a soft tawny color.

Some people believe that the leopard's main food is the baboon. After a lifetime of experience in many parts of Africa, and having kept numerous baboons and several leopards in captivity, I am not convinced that leopards prey that often on these large primates. Of course, they have been known to kill and feed on baboons in the wild, but I feel a troop of baboons would be just too much for a single leopard.

One day our troop of five baboons at Chipangali got out of their cage and were free for several hours. We could not coax them back, whatever we tried. In desperation I decided to use Ingwe. I put a collar round his neck and led him toward the open courtyard where the baboons were playing, thinking that as soon as they saw him they would run for their cage and hide.

When they spotted Ingwe, the five baboons crowded together and all turned to face us. Jacobus, the leader, gave a deep, low bark. This was the signal! The troop attacked, and the leopard and I were surrounded. They made quick lunges at Ingwe, trying to grab or bite him. I yelled and shouted at them, but they ignored me. Hearing the tremendous clamor, four of our assistants arrived with sticks and forced the baboons to retreat. Ingwe and I were more than a little shaken as I walked the terrified leopard back to his cage.

Later when Ingwe was allowed to run loose at Chipangali, the large baboons gathered inside their cage and "attacked" him through the wire. Ingwe loved to climb on top of the cages, and would run from one to the next, but he learned not to get on the wire of the baboon cage. They would hang on the roof and try to bite and grab his feet, crying infuriatingly all the time. The baboons' noise at these times was deafening.

When Ingwe was about, free or on the chain, the other animals all reacted differently. The impala female would snort loudly and bounce about. The little duiker, strangely enough, would try to attack the leopard. The crested crane never hesitated to attack, while the smaller cats, especially the servals, became agitated and retreated into their dens.

Sandy, our lioness, was aloof and unconcerned by Ingwe's presence. If she was lying against the wire in her large open paddock and Ingwe suddenly appeared, she would pretend she had not seen him, although her widening yellow eyes gave the game away.

Sandy and her brother, Joe, were born in captivity, but reared by their mother.

They had not been handled by humans, and were far from tame. When we were offered the cubs, I readily accepted, but when they arrived at Chipangali I learned they were not "small" as I surmised, but rather 18-month-old "large cubs" and completely unmanageable.

While their paddock was being built, the lions were kept in a wire cage. Quite often when I passed the cage I'd stick my fingers through the wire and lightly stroke the animals, trying to get them used to me.

One day in mid-November 1976 I put my right index finger through the wire to scratch Sandy on her shoulder. Suddenly she turned her head and gave me a very severe bite. I yelled in agony as the blood spurted from the long, deep gash.

This was the same finger that developed gangrene after the snake bite two decades before, the one stiffened by an operation, and it had always been sensitive. Now the lioness had bitten through the finger, severing the tendons and nerves. I was taken to the hospital in Bulawayo.

The young doctor in the emergency ward gave me several injections, one to deaden the pain. But the injections and stitching were worse than the bite. Perspiration poured from my face, the pain was so severe.

In the next couple of days the finger got worse and worse. I went to another doctor who removed the stitches from the now badly swollen flesh. He said the wound should never have been stitched.

During this time my own doctor was out of town. When he returned, there had been no improvement; we both agreed that the wise thing to do was to remove the finger. Thus ended the life of a digit that had been the victim of so many bites and scratches from a multitude of wildlife.

Later we had more problems with the two lions. Joe was very aggressive toward Sandy. He hogged the food and dominated the paddock. So when I received a request from a private park for a lion to be used for breeding purposes, I was only too happy to donate Joe, permanently! The only hitch: We had to deliver him, which was not an easy task.

Joe made it very clear that he was not going to do what we wanted — and that was to walk into a large, steel travelling crate. I decided he would have to be drugged, so I mixed my last solution in a syringe. When he came close to the edge of his wire enclosure, I squirted the drug into his partly open mouth. Joe closed his mouth the second the solution touched his tongue; most of it splashed against his canines and dribbled down his lower lip.

He spat and moaned. Globs of saliva formed in his mouth. He should have gone down in 20 minutes, but an hour later he was still staggering around. Since the one dose was all I had, I decided to take a chance and try to walk him to the crate. I told Kevin and Barry to hide. Joe weighed 300 pounds and certainly was not tame. There was no telling what he would do, even though he was still staggering.

As I opened the door, Joe charged at me like a shot from a gun. Then he fell, was up in a second, then fell again. There was just enough drug in his system to prevent a serious attack. The boys came out of their hiding places. Joe growled and spat at us, but his strength was gone. We managed to get him to walk and crawl the six yards into his crate. I let out a heavy sigh of relief.

Paddy, the boys and I drove Joe to his new home. With the crate standing sky-high in the back of our Ranchero, I'm sure we looked like "Chipangali Hillbillies" going down the highway. Reaching the park several hours later, Joe had completely recovered from the effects of the drug, and was released into a beautifully wooded enclosure with his new mate.

The caracal is a very attractive animal. A robustly built cat, it weighs about 30 pounds. The African caracal, often called the lynx, is closely related to the American bobcat and the northern lynx; it has the same ear tufts as the northern lynx but lacks the side whiskers. Its coat is thick, soft and silky. The typical lynx occurring in the Cape Province of South Africa is dark red, whereas the Zimbabwe subspecies is light fawn-colored. The ears and face are the main features of the caracal and give the animal its real beauty.

Caracals flicking their long sharp-tipped and slender ears are a delight to watch. They are often pitch-black with a long tassel of hair. The outside of the ears is covered with silver hair while the inside is light grey. A black spot on either side of the face near the muzzle, and a black line from the eye to the nose, with some white on the chin and at the base of the ear, make the caracal's face one of the most beautiful of the African felines.

In the wild the caracal can tolerate almost any type of country. It loves the open, arid, scrub desert country of the Kalahari in Botswana and Namibia, and is equally at home in dense woodland in eastern Zambia. A caracal is a powerful cat and can kill young antelope and even duiker weighing as much as itself. Its main diet in the wild, however, would more likely be rats and mice, game birds, hares and reptiles. The caracal is almost entirely nocturnal; in 25 years I've seen them out in daylight only three or four times.

I was especially pleased when I was asked to give a home to two half-grown caracals. These were pets which had become too difficult to keep and could not be released into the wild. They arrived in Bulawayo by air in 1975 — a beautiful pair of males. Although they were tame, they refused to be handled.

Later I was sent two adult females which we paired with the males in separate enclosures.

In 1976 we were offered a three-month-old civet kitten. Civets are not uncommon but because they are nocturnal and live in fairly remote places, they are not often seen. I readily agreed to take the little animal, which we named Fungwe. When the black and white long-haired carnivore arrived I was delighted. Although he hated being handled, he was as tame as could be expected and as long as he had the run of the house and my office he was perfectly content.

However, he played a nasty little game that none of the family enjoyed. He would be running round and round the room, then suddenly leap up and bite one of us on the leg or arm. He preferred toes, and if the children or I were sitting barefoot, he would take a nip at a toe and run off squeaking with delight. His teeth were very sharp and he often drew blood. The game amused Fungwe much more than it did us. I could see why his former owner had wanted to find a home for him.

The civet and the genet are not in fact cats as so many people think. Both belong to the same family as the mongoose and should not be called "civet cats" and "genet cats." On the other hand the serval is a true cat and is rightly referred to as a "serval cat."

We are lucky to have all three species at Chipangali and visitors are always interested to note the difference between them. We also have two lovely Selous mongooses, both, alas, males. A farmer digging springhares on his lands in 1974 unearthed them. One had his tail chopped off with a shovel and had a broken leg when he arrived at the orphanage. We named him Stompie and his brother was called Selousi, after the famous hunter, F.C. Selous, who discovered the species.

In time Fungwe, the civet, began to bite more and more, and eventually had to be kept in a cage and let out at regular intervals for exercise. One day I noticed him rubbing his back end against the concrete-block wall of his cage. A large raw sore had developed on each hind leg. I watched him for a few days to see if they would heal naturally, but he continued to rub the wounds until they became the size of a quarter.

Fungwe's ailment highlighted a problem we had at Chipangali. We had spent a lot of money on a large building designed as an animal hospital and nursery. Unfortunately

Tiki snarls his displeasure

Tiki loves attention from Viv

Young caracal

Candy and Scruffy — two of the very tame caracals at Chipangali Wildlife Orphanage

Adult caracal (lynx) at Chipangali

Janet, an adult female serval, has been
at Chipangali for many years

Adult serval at Chipangali

we did not have the money to equip it with suitable hospital cages, operating tables, medicine cabinets, proper lights, etc.

One day a businessman and his wife visited Chipangali with a busload of members of the Friends of Chipangali Society. Before he left he said, "Viv, how much would you require to fit the hospital out?" He took me by surprise. I calculated very quickly and said, "I should think about $3,000." A check for that amount was in the mail within a few days, and within a month the hospital was ready for use.

Our first patient was Fungwe. At last he was in a spotlessly clean cage with new blankets and all the attention he required. After one injection of medicine prescribed by our veterinary surgeon, all other treatment stopped, and his wounds began to heal. Within a fortnight most of the raw areas had closed over with new skin and hair, and he was well on his way to recovery.

A new era had begun for Chipangali.

CHAPTER EIGHTEEN

BABOONS & PORCUPINES

SATURDAYS USUALLY mean a barrage of visitors at Chipangali. On one such afternoon, hearing a burst of laughter, I looked up from my office desk and froze. Sitting on the windowsill was Jacobus — our biggest male baboon.

The whole troop had escaped and they were walking around among the visitors, who, not realizing the danger, were laughing unconcernedly. I opened the door of my office calmly enough, though my knees were knocking, and walked outside as if nothing had happened. The last thing I wanted to do was frighten either the visitors or the baboons. If the animals were frightened or annoyed they could attack with alarming consequences.

The troop consisted of 45-pound Jacobus, the leader; Cheeky, second largest male; and three females, Bambi who was about four years old, and two younger ones. We had had the baboons for some years, and apart from one of the small females, they were a gentle lot. Jacobus fortunately had the best nature, and he was also the greatest clown. He never tried to grab food from one's hands and was usually a most lovable animal.

The baboons always reacted to the different tones of my voice. All I had to do to show I was annoyed or upset was to raise my voice. Had I done that now they would have attacked some of the visitors without hesitation. My very presence could stimulate them to do dangerous things, and because of that I never went near the baboons' cage while the staff was inside washing the floors.

As I walked toward them that afternoon, in a quiet voice I told the visitors to walk very slowly and unobtrusively away from the area, well away from the baboons. I said they should not raise their voices and should keep their children still and silent.

171

The baboons understood quick movements of my arms, for instance a signal that someone should "get out," so I avoided any such gesture. However they always registered as a sign of friendship the movement of my lips, when I emitted a special slight sound. As the visitors moved slowly away, I moved my lips and spoke softly to the baboons. At once Jacobus came bounding up to me and wrapped his arms around my legs, followed by Bambi.

By now the three staff members who looked after the animals had appeared with a dish full of grain, and some was thrown into the cage. Jacobus, Cheeky, Bambi and one of the young females crawled back into their cage through the hole they had made in the wire, and settled down to enjoy the grain. Our handyman quickly arrived to mend the wire. Unfortunately the most aggressive baboon, Nkai, was the one still loose. We tried to coax her back through the cage door for half-an-hour; meanwhile about 30 of the visitors had gathered quite nearby to watch the "fun."

I was still apprehensive and in desperation told the staff that enough was enough and we should catch Nkai with nets. All hell broke loose as we stormed after the frightened baboon. She screamed hysterically, and this set off the other 50 monkeys and baboons at Chipangali. Nkai bounced from one cage to the next and took off into the bush and long grass, closely followed by the staff, yelling with the excitement of the chase. As the baboon scrambled from tree to tree and through the grass, the staff pursued her. At last poor Nkai was trapped in the brush and six eager hands grabbed her. She was returned to her cage with much excitement and chatter from the other baboons at her homecoming. A few minutes later everything was back to normal and the troop settled down to playing and feeding.

The visitors now gathered near the baboon cage and expressed their own versions of what had actually happened. Everyone had thoroughly enjoyed the afternoon's entertainment except Nkai and myself. I do not mind the animals getting out, but not when visitors are about. We cannot afford to take chances.

One of my laborers, David, will never forget another occasion when the five big baboons escaped. As so often happens we managed to get four of them back into the cage. This time, Jacobus decided he was going to stay free. He strutted around like a king, completely unafraid, and making no effort to run away. He filled his cheek pouches with more and more food that he found under the trees. David said he would try to grab him by the tail. I warned him not to, for Jacobus is large and agile, and while it is easy to capture a monkey or a small baboon by the tail, it cannot be done with a large animal.

We became thoroughly frustrated with Jacobus. He obviously had no intention of returning to his cage of his own free will. Once we very nearly got him in but the door was slammed too late and he escaped again. He was annoyed by this and grabbed our handyman by the legs and took several bites at him, and scratched him with his long claws. Fortunately Jacobus had his mouth so full of food that he could not bite, and the man escaped with a few scratches and shallow teeth marks.

Two hours later he was still loose. Then he approached David who caught him by the tail, in spite of my earlier warnings. In retaliation, the baboon swung around and grabbed David's genitals, taking a great bite at them. David screamed in agony and immediately released the tail. The baboon shot off in one direction and David in the other. Screams of laughter and the clapping of hands came from the other Africans as David quickly removed his trousers to inspect the damage. To his intense relief he was still intact and was none the worse for his ordeal. From that time on he kept well clear of operations concerning the baboons, and especially Jacobus. We eventually caught Jacobus with nets and he went back to his cage having enjoyed a pleasant morning's freedom.

One day a young African brought a small sickly baboon to Chipangali. I explained that we did not buy animals, but he said he did not want money, he was just concerned about the little creature and had heard that we might take it in. I was touched that he cared more for the animal than for money. The little baboon was called Orphan Anne, and over the months her condition improved tremendously.

Paddy loved the baboons more than any of the other animals, and she had two favorites. One was Jacobus and the other Jethro, who was brought to Chipangali in November 1974 when he was very small. He could not have been more than a week or two old. His flesh was still very red and his hair pitch-black. He was so tiny that he could not climb out of a shoebox, and Paddy took over rearing him.

She became very attached to Jethro and spent hours playing with him. At first he was fed five times a day on baby food, and he thrived on it. He had a baby's pacifier to suck which kept him happy and he wore a baby's diaper in the interests of hygiene. Jethro had been brought to Chipangali by a Swiss mission engineer in Zimbabwe who got him from a native who was trying to sell him. I was all set to leave for several months on my Antarctic expedition when Jethro arrived and he became a great companion for Paddy during my absence.

One day many years later we noticed that Jethro was struggling to get something out of his mouth; it was obviously irritating him a great deal. He kept sticking his fingers into his mouth and pushing at whatever was stuck between his teeth. This went on for several days and it seemed to be getting worse. He became reluctant to eat and something was obviously needing our attention.

In Jethro's cage were a number of wooden poles for the animals to swing and play on, and to chew on to keep their teeth in shape. I had often seen Jethro chewing pieces of wood from the poles and I thought the problem could be a splinter between his teeth or in the gums. To investigate we would have to immobilize him completely and have a good look in his mouth.

This incident occurred during the filming of the TV series "Orphans of the Wild" and we decided to film the entire operation. We had to get Jethro into a large "squeeze cage" and then inject him. He was such an affectionate animal that we had no problem coaxing him into a cage where he was given the drug. In no time he was fast asleep.

We then removed him from the cage and examined his mouth. Sure enough, there was a large splinter stuck solidly between two teeth. We managed to remove the offending piece of wood with forceps and in due course, Jethro came around and was moved back to his cage to join the females.

He was none the worse for his little operation and we were pleased that we were able to help him. The incident made an interesting segment in the TV series. Although Jethro was loved and well cared for, and treated as a child, at a year old he was unmanageable and we could no longer let him run around freely. He would bite if anyone tried to grab him or punish him for bad behavior. As with so many other wild animals, baboons are fun to have around when young and cuddly, but as they grow older they become a great nuisance and are difficult to keep. That is the time when many pet owners turn to us. In the first three years at Chipangali, we had more than 30 baboons brought in to the orphanage, nearly all ex-pets.

———————

A taxi pulled up in front of the museum in Bulawayo one day, and on the back seat was an unusual passenger. It was not the type normally expected to travel in a taxi-cab — a vervet monkey. The driver produced a letter which read:

Dear Mr. Wilson,
   Herewith one vervet monkey. Know you will give her a home and not destroy her. Sorry no money for a donation.

I asked the driver where he had gotten the monkey and letter, and he said a lady had asked him what the fare was to the museum. She then gave him 50 cents and said, "Take this animal to Mr. Wilson."

"Taxi," as she was named, was a bad-tempered young female, perhaps 18 months old, with a very light-colored coat compared with our other vervet monkeys. She had a strap around her waist and had been chained up for some time. Raw and festering

174

Adult samango (blue) monkey

Jethro, a baby chacma baboon

wounds showed where the strap had cut into her flesh. It was no wonder that the poor creature was bad tempered.

When I tried to remove the strap, she promptly let me know how painful it was and how much she distrusted humans by giving me two quick bites. I left her alone until we got to Chipangali. There I got Packson, my senior assistant, to hold her while I cut the leather strap off her and treated her wounds. Had she been able to speak I know she would have thanked me; her sad eyes said as much. Taxi was placed in a small cage where it was easy to catch and treat her, and where I could see how her wounds were healing.

In the meantime several more vervet monkeys arrived at Chipangali, so altogether we had five newcomers ready to be introduced to the older residents. If I had suddenly put a single, strange monkey straight into the enclosure with the dozen old-timers, the intruder would be chased about and bitten so badly that it would eventually be killed. To introduce primates to one another, the newcomers are first put into a small cage, and this is placed as close as possible to the cage where they are going, and left there for several weeks. The monkeys become accustomed to one another through the wire and when they are put together there is less fighting than without the familiarization process.

Even so, in this case they still fought a lot and in the process many, if not all, of the new arrivals showed signs of being "beaten up" by the residents. Unfortunately, even if a new arrival is bitten and bleeding, it has to be left in the cage for its wounds to heal naturally — unless the wound is very severe, in which case the monkey is removed. When a wounded monkey is taken out of a cage, it is very difficult to re-introduce it. When five or six newcomers are introduced at the same time, they all have a better chance, and in the confusion many escape without injury.

More people in Zimbabwe have monkeys as pets than any other wild animal and this species causes the greatest trouble. As soon as they mature they begin to bite and can be extremely dangerous. Then the owners have to get rid of them. Some bring them to Chipangali, and are good enough to give a donation toward their upkeep; some take the animals to a veterinary surgeon and have them destroyed; others merely dump them in the bush and hope that they will fend for themselves. Of those that are released, some find their way to other humans and become a nuisance. Or they die in the wild, either of starvation or killed by predators or other wild monkeys.

One Sunday morning a car pulled up at Chipangali and stopped for a second in the parking lot; the door opened and out jumped a monkey. The driver slammed the door and drove off in a cloud of dust. Our tea garden is close to the car lot and the vervet monkey made his way to a crowd of visitors. He decided he would like

Paddy with young chacma baboons

a slice of cake which was being eaten by a child. Someone tried to chase it away and it promptly bit the child on the arm. I was immediately called, not only to render first-aid treatment but also to capture the monkey — which had taken to the uppermost branches of a large fig tree.

The child had to be taken to the hospital for anti-tetanus and penicillin injections, and I spent several hours trying to get the monkey out of the tree. All of this anxiety and inconvenience was caused by a thoughtless person who was not prepared to hand the monkey over in a decent manner, or perhaps wished to avoid his responsibility for the animal's upkeep at the orphanage.

As this is written, we are planning to release a whole troop of monkeys into the wild in the near future. They are already being trained to survive on wild fruits, leaves and grass so that when they are eventually released the wild food will not be new to them. They are also being kept without food for a day or more at a time, to help them survive in the harsh environment in which they will find themselves. Already the individuals of the troop are dependent on one another and prefer each other's company to that of humans.

When they are free they will not, we hope, seek human company, or try to join up with a wild troop. The troop to be released consists of 21 animals and many of them are already in breeding condition. Taxi, one of the troop, produced her own baby in captivity, and the others soon learned to help look after it. Several other females are also pregnant. The release area will be chosen with great care. We want to introduce them to a territory not occupied by other monkeys or close to human habitation.

———

Everything seems to happen at Chipangali on Sundays. Early one Sunday morning a gentleman arrived with Togo, a most beautiful white-nosed monkey. The man had recently moved from Zaire to Zimbabwe and brought his pet with him. He asked whether we would look after it for a couple of weeks while he applied for permits to export it to South Africa. That was years ago. We are happy to say that Togo is still with us; his owner never returned.

Toppie, an adorable mona monkey, was a pet in Nigeria — his owner was transferred to Zimbabwe. Soon after his arrival the man had to move to another country and brought Toppie to us. He loved his pet very much and left money to cover her feeding expenses for many months. Toppie and Togo are now together in a cage of their own; they are extremely intelligent forest monkeys and far more attractive and responsive than the vervets.

Other primates that we get from time to time are night-apes and bush babies. Night-

Victoria, the porcupine

The author with two staff members treating a sick chacma baboon

apes, often referred to as nagapies, are common in Matabeleland, and many people keep them. However, they have an unpleasant habit of urinating on their hands, and they become very smelly. As soon as the animals start biting, the owners bring them to Chipangali. While the little night-ape can be a delightful pet to have around the house, its big brother, the bush baby, leaves a lot to be desired. When they become adult they have very long, sharp canines and will think nothing of inflicting nasty bites. I once saw a photographer very badly bitten by a large bush baby.

———————

While I was mammalogist at the museum, a farmer brought in two baby porcupines. They had been washed out of an irrigation pipe. I was delighted with the little creatures and promised to rear them if I could. Porcupines make interesting pets although they weigh about 40 pounds when fully grown. They are the largest of the African rodents.

I took the tiny spiny balls home. Next day the little female died, and I was more determined than ever to raise the male. Although only about two weeks old, he was a really cheeky little devil. He strutted around and stamped his hind feet when annoyed, grunting loudly. My sons asked so often why he stamped his feet that I eventually named him *Chafukwa*, which means "why" in ChiNyanja. Barry and Kevin spent hours playing with Chafukwa, allowing him the run of the lawn where he ate grass-roots and any other vegetation he could find.

At first his quills were soft, and he could be handled without difficulty. As he got older they became solid and hard. He weighed 20 ounces when he arrived at the museum, and was fed twice a day on undiluted cow's milk and porridge. When weaned he was eating potatoes, carrots and other vegetables, and loved grass-roots and wild berries. At two months, he was kept permanently outdoors in a large cage made of bird-wire, but he often chewed holes in it and came to the back door of the house wanting to be let in.

At three months Chafukwa weighed five pounds and was growing at an alarming rate. We had not then established Chipangali, so Chafukwa was given to the Bulawayo Municipality, and kept in a large aviary with a flock of birds as companions. He immediately began demolishing the wire sides of the aviary which had to be constantly repaired. The cage looked a real mess as a result of his digging and gnawing habits.

Later, Paddy and I received a lovely female porcupine, which we called Victoria. At Chipangali she was one of the first to move into her new cage, built of concrete blocks and frames of heavy diamond-mesh wire. At first she rattled the frames for hours until they broke loose and had to be rebuilt more strongly.

Vervet monkeys — Taxi is the one on the pole

Then Victoria chewed steadily at one particular place in a wire-frame until she broke through the wire, making a small hole about an inch in diameter. The hole was repaired. She attacked the same spot again and made another hole. This process of Victoria making holes and us repairing them continued for years until the area repaired was about six inches by a foot.

I awoke at 2:00 A.M. one morning and heard a strange noise outside our bedroom window. I lay still for a few minutes and as I listened I was sure it was a porcupine rushing about, as if playing a game on the lawn. I sneaked out of bed and tiptoed to the window. There, dancing about on the grass, was Victoria. She rushed about, backward and forward, rattling her tail quills. Every now and then she stopped and reversed a short distance, stepped sideways and continued her game. The moon was so bright I could clearly see all that was going on. She was thoroughly enjoying her solo dance in the moonlight.

It was July and midwinter and very cold but I always slept only in my underpants. I rushed outside just as I was and opened the large door of Victoria's cage. I then tried, desperately, to drive her into it. Each time I got close to her she turned her back to me, and with erected quills, moved in reverse toward me, her tail vibrating violently. These sudden stops were hazardous, for I ran the chance of impaling myself on her quills, with painful consequences. The large quills, hollow and tubular, are extremely hard and sharp, and can inflict serious wounds which usually become infected. Lions and other predators have often been found with broken porcupine quills embedded in suppurating quill wounds.

Victoria moved about with short swift rushes, uttering loud grunts. We were still outside the bedroom window, and making a tremendous noise. I was sure Paddy had been awakened, and I yelled for her to come and help. I knocked on the window but there was no response. She was obviously dreaming contentedly and in no mood to be chasing a porcupine at 3:00 A.M., in the middle of winter.

Since there was no chance of getting Victoria in her cage by myself, I raced across the bush to the staff houses, nearly half a mile, barefooted — and still in my underpants. I banged on the doors of four rooms and soon six of the staff trotted back to the animal area with me. They were dressed much as I was. One had only a blanket wrapped around him. When we got back to the area, Victoria had disappeared. She had retreated into some brush and rocks, under a very large wild fig tree close to the animal cages.

I tore into the house for a flashlight. As so often happens in emergencies, the only light had no batteries. I was most annoyed, for presumably one of my sons had removed them for some model or other. I cursed as I ran back into the winter night.

My helpers had located Victoria and they were driving her back to her cage with long sticks, yelling with laughter. The one with only a blanket had hooked it on a thorn-tree and, battling in the nude to recover it, was keeping a wary eye on Victoria's quills.

She walked along slowly, closely followed by us, all nearly naked. We got her safely back into her cage, repaired the damaged wire-frame, and at 3:30 A.M., all returned to bed. As I crawled in beside Paddy she mumbled something about my being cold and had I been out of bed again?

I rose regularly between 1:00 and 2:00 A.M. for a nightly patrol around Chipangali to see that all was well. Early wakening and wandering was a routine I readily accepted, and the cold did not affect me. I was always asleep within minutes after returning to bed.

Victoria was a pleasing animal in spite of her bad habits and nocturnal wanderings. She was a great favorite with the visitors. The question asked most frequently about porcupines is, "Does it shoot its quills at people?" I am certain that it does not, but I do know that if a porcupine is annoyed or frightened, and its skin tenses over its back with the quills erect, loose quills will drop out, or even "shoot" out a short distance.

The flesh of a porcupine is palatable and tender. I often ate it in the Luangwa Valley in Zambia. The tribes living there frequently hunt the animals and the meat roasted over an open fire is truly tasty. I dreaded the thought of releasing Victoria into the wild, for I feared she would be speared and roasted as a delicacy.

Over the years I have received dozens of telephone calls from people around Bulawayo asking how to rear and feed baby porcupines. I always ask the same questions: How big is the baby? What do its quills look like? Where was it found?

The answers are usually predictable. It is a little larger than a man's fist. It has short spines or quills, nearly an inch long. It was found walking in the garden. Occasionally someone would say that it was brought in by his dog. With this evidence, the little animal is not a porcupine, I would explain, but an adult hedgehog.

A hedgehog is not a rodent, as is the porcupine, but an insectivore. In other words, it feeds on insects and meaty substances and not plant material, as the porcupine does. It is interesting that two mammals can be so alike externally, and yet anatomically so very different. The little hedgehog belongs to the order of primitive mammals. It has short limbs, a longish snout and many teeth adapted for crushing and grasping insects and other hard foods on which it feeds.

The spiny little chap makes a delightful pet. When afraid it rolls into a tight ball and the sharp, hard spines protect face, legs and soft underparts. Once it has become accustomed to people it rarely rolls up and will even take insects and pieces of meat from the hand. The habitat around Bulawayo is ideal for hedgehogs; there are probably more in and around the city than anywhere else in southern or central Africa.

During Chipangali's first four years we had 20 to 30 hedgehogs brought in annually, always between August and March. As soon as it starts getting cold the little chaps hide away and rest until the temperature goes up in September, or occasionally as early as August.

I have examined many dead hedgehogs, killed on the roads by vehicles, and they nearly always had a thick layer of yellow fat under the skin. This fatty tissue helps keep them alive over the long, cold winter. If hedgehogs are kept indoors in a warm room they will feed all through winter and not curl up and hibernate as they do in the wild. Actually hedgehogs do not truly hibernate in southern Africa as they do in Europe, but I think they become rather more lethargic. As temperatures go down so the state of torpidity increases.

CHAPTER NINETEEN

BLIND DUIKER & BABY ELEPHANTS

NO ONE WILL ever know how long she had battled to get through the barbed wire cattle-fence that stretched for miles along the main Bulawayo Plumtree Road. Her face and legs were scarlet where the vicious wire had torn her soft, tawny skin. Blood had clotted on several wounds. A young man travelling in western Zimbabwe spotted the duiker on the roadside. He slowed so as not to frighten her and noticed that she was behaving in a most unusual manner. There was something very strange. She kept bumping into the fence and looking from side to side as if she was blind.

He jumped out of his car and ran to grab her. She screamed with fright, kicked and almost ripped his flesh with her razor-sharp hooves. The little duiker, weighing only about 35 pounds, was very determined and powerful. The man staggered back to his car with the kicking and screaming mini-antelope. Then he noticed that both of her eyes were glazed white. She was indeed blind!

Driving while holding the kicking, screaming animal was a nightmare, but he got home at last, and released it into a fenced garden. Then the Samaritan phoned Paddy to ask whether we could take her at Chipangali; of course her answer was yes.

I was in Bulawayo at the depot where injured and sick animals were brought. Two young men arrived in the middle of the busy city street with a duiker wrapped in a blanket, screaming its head off. A crowd gathered immediately. People were very touched by the pathetic sight of the poor blind creature. We named her Marula and put her into a newly built cage, one of a series of six reception-cages provided by the Friends of Chipangali.

A thick layer of soft grass covered the cage floor. She crashed her head against the wire sides for a while, but soon settled down very peacefully. Within 24 hours she knew where the wire was, and from then on she never touched it again.

After two days at Chipangali, Marula started eating fruit and lots of natural vegetation. Leaves of trees and other plants that she would normally have eaten in the wild were also given to her. En route to Chipangali I discovered another interesting thing; she was obviously pregnant and her udder was already well developed. I wanted to avoid causing her undue stress, so did not examine her very closely. I had an eye-specialist check her from a distance, and Chipangali's veterinarian agreed that we should wait until she had produced her baby before considering a detailed examination.

As time passed she became more and more friendly and would even take fruit from my hand. She grew to know instantly the sound of my voice. In the next cage was a male steenbok with a damaged and badly swollen front foot, and he and Marula soon became great friends. Paddy and I reared many duiker at Chipangali since the orphanage's inception; indeed, it was a duiker lamb that first set me thinking about an animal orphanage, in Zambia, way back in 1954. I have a very great love for the species.

When Marula gave birth to a healthy male that spring, we quickly realized that the baby would have to be taken from her. Her blindness prevented her from caring for the infant, and we were afraid she would injure it in some way. We reared the little duiker by hand and it was eventually released on a nearby farm.

Marula, unfortunately, was never cured of her blindness. Our veterinary surgeon did examine her after the baby arrived and found that her situation could not be corrected. She died the following year of an unknown cause. For the time that she was kept at the orphanage, we tried our best to make the dark world around her a little brighter.

In addition to the seven duiker we now have in pens at Chipangali, we have released another 10 onto our 100-acre farm, and I have returned others to the wild in the Matopo Hills and on various farms — not all successfully, I regret to say.

Compared with duiker, steenbok are much more difficult to rear and keep in captivity; we have had more losses with them than with any other species. They thrive for weeks and even months, and then, for some unknown reasons, suddenly die, or take fright and run into a fence or brick wall and kill themselves. We have also released several steenbok on our farm and they appear to thrive on a small property provided they are not harassed by dogs.

Paddy had a steenbok female whom she loved a great deal, named Sandy. It would run around her in tight circles at tremendous speed. Every few minutes Sandy would return to where she was sitting, then suddenly stop and rub herself against Paddy.

It came when called, and Paddy and Sandy were great friends. One sad day we had a torrential storm at Chipangali. Sandy took refuge in a hole made for the warthogs, and the heavy rain filled it with water, drowning her.

On another occasion a steenbok male ran into a fence and broke its neck during a rain and thunderstorm, although there were plenty of places for it to hide and shelter. These little animals do take fright, and tragedy strikes them all too often.

Late one evening in Hwange National Park, about this period, Paddy, Barry and I were in the Land-Rover watching game drinking at Nyamandhlovu Pan. Particularly in the dry season, high concentrations of animals surround these stretches of water in the early morning and in the evening. We had seen giraffe, zebra, kudu, water-buck, jackal and a bull elephant during the hour we spent there.

There were four crocodiles in the water. One, popularly known as "Beadle" after a former judge and big-game hunter, was very large. There were also two hippo, a mother and her rather frolicsome baby. He was forever half out of the water chomping away at something, for all the world like any modern teen-ager chewing incessantly on bubble gum. Every now and again the bouncing baby hippo would submerge and then surface noisily, splashing and making waves.

Mother and son were at our end of the pan. Then a herd of 12 buffalo emerged from the thick bush at the other bank and began to march majestically to the water's edge. When the whole herd was lined up in the shallow water to drink, the baby hippo swam straight toward the great beasts. Mother appeared unconcerned, although there was a very big crocodile basking on the shore nearby.

When it reached the drinking buffalo, the baby hippo stood up as if to greet them. Some buffalo reversed cautiously from the precocious infant, but the little hippo waddled on toward them. He was so small in relation to them he could easily have passed under the bellies of the buffalo, which meant he could not have been more than two feet high. One of their massive horns could have ripped the baby hippo to bloody ribbons. But it moved steadily forward and, as it reached each animal, buffalo and baby hippo touched noses, sniffing each other. The baby did the rounds, going from one buffalo to the next, like a small boy, home from school, politely greeting each elderly relation.

Once, when three or four buffalo moved forward together to sniff and inspect, the baby opened its cavernous mouth and the big animals backed off. The hippo then took a mud bath and if the buffalo became too inquisitive, he opened those great jaws again and the buffalo politely withdrew. At no time was there any aggression. None of the animals ever seemed agitated or afraid. All was peace and tranquility. Suddenly Mama hippo, from the middle of the pan, gave a loud snort, signalling the end of the fraternization. Like a chubby high-powered motorboat, the calf plunged into the water and streamed back to his mother's side.

―――――

Back at Chipangali an old friend phoned to say he had found a newly born kudu calf trapped in a barbed wire fence on a farm about 50 miles from Bulawayo. One of its hind legs had been bitten by jackals while it was in the wire. Less than a week old, its umbilical cord was still wet and red, and it weighed only 41 pounds.

Paddy named her Suzie, and she grew into a fine young lady. Most of her day was spent walking around her paddock, which she shared with ostriches, duiker, steenbok and other animals, feeding on acacia leaves and pods. Each afternoon she went for a fast run, galloping round the paddock at a great pace and scattering all before her. The guinea-fowl yelled indignantly at her behavior, and the male ostriches spread their great black wings and ran helter-skelter in all directions. The duiker and steenbok hid in the long grass to keep out of her way. After about 20 circuits Suzie would stop, have a drink from the natural pan in the paddock, and settle down to feed again.

―――――

One Sunday afternoon I saw a man approaching the office with an animal on a lead. I thought it was a dog and was about to warn him that no pets were allowed at Chipangali, but as he got closer I saw that it was a baby impala. It was most unusual to see a young antelope in a harness. The owner explained that he had found the baby beside the railway line in the bush, and as he was sure it was lost, or abandoned by its mother, he took it home. He kept her for a week and named her Sham, but feeling that he could not raise her in town, brought her to Chipangali.

She grew into a beautiful animal with a smooth soft coat and was always meticulously clean and shiny. If I was near, she would never leave my side. It was almost impossible to get a good photograph of her for she insisted on looking into the lens of my camera and licking it, coating it with saliva. She lived with several duiker in a separate paddock, between the warthogs' enclosure and the crested cranes' area, and she, too, loved *pronking*, as the springbok does, throwing her hind legs high into the air as she bounced along, almost like a four-legged ballet dancer.

―――――

Over the years I have seen many baby elephants in captivity. Most of them died if, when captured, they were shorter than about four feet at the shoulder. I had several in Zambia and often wished I could get another baby, but of course I would not

188

Suzie the kudu
at one week old

"Sham" — one of the many impala at Chipangali Wildlife Orphanage

deliberately take one from the wild. However, if one became available, I would always be ready to give it a home at Chipangali.

The opportunity came in 1975 on the occasion of an elephant-culling operation in Hwange National Park. This involves the killing of an overpopulation of several thousand elephant. There was usually a demand for female elephant babies, but very few zoos wanted males. So the young females were captured and sold to animal dealers for about $600 while the little males were destroyed.

I approached the Department of Wildlife Management, offering a home for one of the baby males. They agreed, and I was soon advised that a baby was ready for me to fetch from the park. We built a strong pole-stockade. The warden in charge of the park had offered the loan of a crate for transporting the elephant, but when my sons and I reached the game park, we learned the warden had just left for Bulawayo. Despite our search, we could not find the crate. I also learned that the smallest of the 20 baby elephants, and the only one not feeding, was the one destined for Chipangali. It looked very sick.

In a way I was grateful for the mix-up over the crate, because it delayed the move. I felt that if the baby was left with the other elephants for a while it would be more likely to try to feed. The rangers agreed to look after it for a couple of weeks.

That night my boys and I camped near the elephant pens, happy to be sleeping under the stars in wild country, with no tents or other comforts. Sounds of elephant and hyena surrounded us. Suddenly lions roared close to camp. The boys quickly put more wood on the fire. The natives who were looking after the elephants did the same, to give themselves courage and to keep the lions away from the tiny elephant calves. Barry's eyes nearly popped out of his head and shone in the light of the campfire. We tried to estimate how close the prowlers were. For once Kevin had nothing to say.

At dawn the next day we drove around the game reserve and saw several herds of elephant, many impala and kudu, a large herd of a couple of hundred buffalo and about 25 giraffe. We also watched a black-backed jackal carrying a guinea-fowl. At one of the pans was a big male baboon with a three-inch open gash in his cheek; the bones of his face and his teeth were visible through the torn flesh. Presumably the wound had been inflicted by another male in a fight, or by a predator, perhaps a leopard. The boys were most impressed when they saw two large kudu bulls fighting. We watched them for some time before they parted and went their separate ways into the thick bush.

Our little elephant's mother had been shot in the Gomo area of the park and we felt "Gomo" would be an apt name for him. Upon our return to Chipangali I had a special crate made that fitted neatly into the back of my Ranchero. It was a well-

A newly born common grey duiker

The same duiker at 3½ years old

constructed crate that could be used to move other animals later. Paddy and I then made the second trip to collect Gomo. At the elephant camp it was sad to see Gomo being pushed around by the other baby elephants. He really was a lot smaller than the rest. The game ranger in charge estimated that Gomo was about three years old but I had my own views. I could not see how, at just under three feet high, he could be more than a year old.

A German animal-trader, Jurgen, who had come to Hwange to collect all the other baby elephants, agreed. Jurgen was very experienced and felt the little chap was not more than 10 to 12 months old, and far from weaned. Jurgen had been living at the camp with the elephants, preparing crates to transport them to Europe, and had Gomo feeding on a calf-substitute milk. He was not happy about Gomo's condition and felt we would be lucky if we reared him successfully.

Gomo was eventually loaded into his crate, and along with two members of my staff, we set off for home, packed to capacity. We stopped frequently to ensure that Gomo was all right. When we reached the orphanage late in the afternoon, with the help of a dozen men, we lifted Gomo and the crate from the truck, and he was introduced to his new home.

At first he disliked everything. He charged about screaming with outstretched ears, and even tried to ram me against the poles of his stockade. It took several days to quiet him down. After only a week he was tame enough to cuddle and stroke, but he lost a lot of weight because of his change of diet.

During the second week, Gomo was let out of his stockade and allowed to wander about, but with an attendant accompanying him at all times. He loved to have me squeeze him, and if I pinched him gently behind the front legs, he would squeal with approval. Sometimes he would playfully rumble away when I spoke to him. He was such a lovable and affectionate animal it was hard to believe he was not a domestic pet. I ended up becoming as fond of Gomo as any other animal I ever had. Over the 25 years that I had been rearing wild creatures, totaling at least a couple of hundred ranging from elephant to bats, I had never known one as affectionate as Gomo.

From the time we got him, however, we had problems. At first he was constipated, and then he had diarrhea. I battled to cure the runny-tummy which lasted for days at a time. Then a veterinarian from Harare suggested I use rice-water and glucose. This did the trick and after that, whenever he got diarrhea, we fed him this mixture.

Gomo became very bloated at times, and this was also a worry. I would push my fist hard against his stomach, not actually punching him, and in this way gas that had built up would be expelled. Every day it seemed, something new went wrong with the lovable little chap, and how sad I felt for him. One day he was up and about

Kevin with Gomo the baby elephant

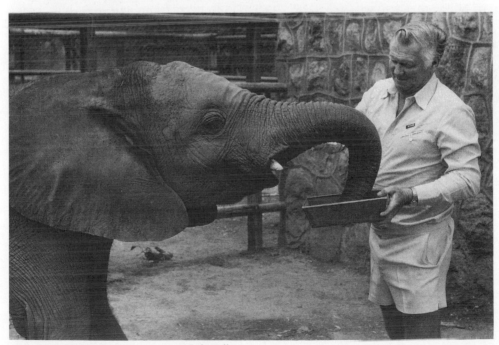

Viv feeds the baby elephant "Mukwa"

and running, and the next day he could hardly walk.

One day in October 1975, the temperature in Bulawayo suddenly dropped to almost freezing. That night the temperature stayed low and the next morning Gomo could hardly move. He had a severe case of pneumonia and was having great difficulty breathing. From time to time thick mucous was blown out of his trunk. We moved him from his stockade to a log cabin in which the children normally played.

As he lay on a thick mat of soft grass, he was rubbed all over by several of our staff to warm him up and increase circulation. We also covered him with a thick woolen blanket and hung two infrared lights over him. He was given shots of penicillin and streptomycin in the hindquarters. Even when the sharp needle penetrated his thick hide he barely moved. He received constant nursing all that day, and by late afternoon he managed, with help, to get to his feet. He staggered about slowly on trembling legs and he looked so unhappy. That night an attendant slept with him, and I also spent most of the night by his side. All the following week he was closely watched, and kept warm day and night. I think I averaged less than three hours sleep a day.

After 10 days his pneumonia cleared up and we all sighed with relief. By this time I was exhausted, and longed for a good night's sleep. Poor Gomo's hindquarters were so sore where he had been getting injections that he refused to let me touch him.

The weather warmed up and he was moved to his outdoor stockade; but he did not like it there. He always looked unhappy, and when I visited him he would scream with delight and rub himself against me as if I were some favorite scratching-pole. He would take my hand in his trunk and gently put it into his mouth. He loved the comfort of softly sucking my fingers, and I am sure he felt I was his mother and his security. As long as I was with him he would eat whatever I gave him, and he strutted about happily. As soon as I walked away, he became restless and sad. Unfortunately I could not spend all my time with Gomo, much as I would have loved to. There was a lot going on at Chipangali and many other animals needed attention.

Because of Gomo's pneumonia and his bad circulation, the edges of his ears became dry, and in places, raw and red. Then sores developed. The government veterinarian looked at him and advised he be given sunflower oil to drink and to rub on his body. He seemed to like the oil; there was no problem getting him to drink it and he started to improve immediately.

Next, his hind legs were a problem. We noticed that they clicked in a jerky manner as he walked, and appeared weak. We suspected rickets. We gave him calcium and vitamin D daily, but there was little change. Sometimes he had great difficulty getting up after a long nap; on some occasions, though, he would almost bounce to his feet.

To our great distress it became obvious that Gomo was getting weaker. He was moved back to the log cabin where the infrared lights were kept on him all night. He was again covered with blankets, and watched day and night.

Although weak, he was allowed to walk about, and on hot days he was given a bath and washed down. He loved a mud bath. After lying in the cool, red mud for some time he would get up and cover himself with dry sand, picking up small quantities with his trunk and blowing it over himself, or throwing it onto his back. He would then go to his favorite tree and rub himself against it. He appeared happy at these times but I could see he was not well. Visitors to Chipangali thought he was looking fine but I knew better.

One sad day Gomo just could not stand up. He lay on his side moaning. Several of us tried to lift him to his feet but his legs buckled under him and he rested on his brisket and tummy. After a time we rolled him over on his side. He was dying, and oh, so slowly. I had watched my other two baby elephants succumb in the same way. I felt so helpless and desperate. I felt I should put him away, but loved him so much that as long as he was alive and breathing, I felt there was still some hope.

Gradually the life went out of him, ending a truly wonderful friendship. Perhaps I should have let him be shot when his mother was shot, but then I was sure in my thoughts that if another baby elephant needed help, I would do it all again.

The magnificent African elephant possesses highly evolved social habits, and exceptional intelligence. It has intense family loyalties, and that incredible fifth limb — powerful, flexible and sensitive — the trunk. It is also blessed with monumental size, and an appetite to match. Elephants both in zoos and in the wild are more loved and, perhaps, more studied and respected, than all of Africa's rich kaleidoscope of wildlife.

In Zimbabwe's wild areas and national parks, there are healthy, young and expanding elephant populations with a very high birth rate — and most reach adulthood. In fact Zimbabwe elephants have increased to the extent that in some places they have become a threat to other animal populations. There are now, perhaps, ten times as many elephants in Zimbabwe as there were at the turn of the century.

In 1980, there were some 40,000 elephants in the country, and it is estimated that 20,000 have been shot in the last 20 years. The great herds have a most catholic diet and consume vegetation with such vigor that they have become, after man, the most important modifying influence on the habitats in Africa. Their destructive and wasteful feeding habits are exemplified by the many large trees ring-barked and often destroyed by them, when they want only small fragments of the inner bark, which they find a delicacy. In this way many trees well over 100 years old are destroyed in a very short time. These giants will also often push over large trees, merely to sample some tidbit of foliage — or to get at the highly palatable seedpods out of reach.

If elephants become too numerous in the areas where they are protected, they become a major problem and destroy the habitat on which many other animals depend. Yet the long-lived species must be protected to maintain stability in the ecosystem. If eland or zebra with life spans of 15 years qualify as long-lived species, even the great elephant which lives to about 60 fills only a passing moment in time compared to the ancient ebony and baobab trees in our valuable woodland.

Zimbabwe could lose 75 percent of its zebra and eland in the national parks, and in about 10 to 20 years would recover by natural breeding. However, if 75 percent of our main tree species were destroyed and lost, the habitats would be damaged beyond short-term recovery, and with their destruction a wide range of lesser animal species such as kudu, sable, tsessebe, roan antelope and a good many others would also be lost.

However, if we protect and manage our habitats successfully, the wide variety of mammals and other animals that inhabit them will, by and large, look after themselves. Because elephants have a phenomenal ability to alter or destroy vast areas of natural vegetation, there are very few plants and animals which escape their influence.

Severe damage to woodlands can be seen near elephant paths leading to water holes and pans, and their constant use inevitably transforms the woodland into desert. If this is allowed to happen, many rare and endangered species, such as roan antelope or black rhino, could be lost forever, even though the woodland itself could recover eventually. If Zimbabwe's national parks' staff is to continue to manage wildlife areas for rare species, it will be hopeless unless the elephant problem is solved first.

Leading ecologists maintain that species are far more important than individual animals or plants, and that biological communities are more important than species. In fact, entire ecosystems are more important than their constituent communities.

From these basic principles, it is obvious that it is the wildlife habitats which must be preserved — that is, the vegetation itself on which so many species depend. In Zimbabwe, the major ecological problem for wildlife managers are those relating to elephants, fire, and water supplies. Of these, the elephant problem is the most controversial because it involves the reduction of elephant populations.

A cattleman on a vast ranch who keeps his cattle until they reach old age, will suffer the ravages of overgrazing. By the same token national parks managers need to crop wild animals to preserve the habitat. However, professional wildlife ecologists are by no means unanimous about the answer to the elephant population problem. What is not disputed is that with all the protection man is giving elephants, there are pockets of overpopulation; what should be done, and how to do it, is the question.

There are two schools of thought. One is to "let nature take its course." The over-crowded species will eat itself out of house and home, and therefore die off in large numbers, eventually resting the land and allowing it to recover.

The second option is an active range management plan to control animal numbers, to minimize habitat destruction. The first option, to let the animals die naturally in a desolation of bare ground and barren trees, is unthinkable. This is not feasible in a land of protein-hungry people — not to mention the deliberate destruction of the land.

The Zimbabwe parks research staff has a program which entails "culling," or as some people call it, "population reduction," of elephants, which is essential if the vegetation is to be kept in a sound, balanced condition.

On one such exercise in August 1978, a team of nine men did the culling, assisted by an aircraft pilot, a research officer and five specialist "skinners" to recover the meat, skins and bones from the dead elephants. There was another gang of 250 to help cut up and process the meat. The operations camp at Ngweshla Pan looked like a vast army depot with dozens of vehicles, tractors, a trailer, two airplanes, many tents and hundreds of people, all essential for a quick and efficient operation.

On the day I arrived 35 elephant had been shot and four babies captured. That night the campfire was well-ventilated with stories of the operation, from a dozen different viewpoints, and varying accounts of what each man felt during the day.

Next morning the pilot returned from a dawn patrol with a report of two herds of elephant about 15 miles south of camp. The culling column set out to find them. I was in the first open Land-Rover with seven game rangers and eight gun bearers. All 16 of us clung to the vehicle as it bounced along the bush-track. Another open Land-Rover followed with two wardens and 14 assistants adorned with ropes, and carrying boxes of immobilizing drugs, Capchur guns, spare rifles, food and water. Then came the research team with more assistants, and yet another Land-Rover with more people. At the tail of the convoy the 10-ton truck wallowed along slowly, with three large wooden crates for baby elephants, then a string of tractors and trailers each piled full of more helpers. The convoy covered several miles.

As we approached the elephants the aircraft pilot radioed directions and reported the herd about three miles ahead. We stopped to make final plans, and then "bush-bashed" toward the herd. The pilot in the light aircraft was observing the scene below and kept us informed by radio.

We bashed through the bush in deep Kalahari sand. Our vehicle suddenly came to an abrupt halt as the right rear spring dug into the earth. The "U" bolts had sheared (not surprising with our load of 16 people). More re-organization, and I found myself in the second Land-Rover. The team with the drug boxes and ropes followed on foot.

"Just ahead now," radioed the pilot. We offloaded and moved ahead on foot in three teams. Two wardens went to the left, two to the right and the remainder in the center. We were stalking carefully now, to within 35 yards. On a signal the firing began. In a few minutes the entire herd of 23 elephants was shot — except for two male babies, small enough to capture.

The frightened calves were so confused that they remained behind the pile of dead elephants. The capture team moved in. The larger of the little orphans was shot in the buttocks with a drug-dart and down he went. The smaller calf was manhandled and roped. The drugged baby was immediately covered with fresh, green branches and leaves of one of the area's teak trees — known to the Africans as *Muchibi* — to keep him cool and protect his eyes from the sun. Naturally, I called him Muchibi.

The other baby was named "Mukwa" after another of the hardwood trees in the area. Poor little Mukwa put up a strenuous fight, screaming and struggling as he was held down and his legs tied together with ropes.

What a devastating and pathetic sight to see those beautiful baby elephants lying beside that great mass of dead animals. They were indeed "Orphans of the Wild." We humans had created the national parks to protect the elephants. Now as a result of that protection, we had to shoot them to protect other animals and the vegetation.

The operation was absolutely essential. It was properly planned by first-class ecologists; it was no haphazard affair. Whole herds of elephant had to be removed to create a sort of vacuum where, later, other elephants could take their place. I knew it had to be done. There was no other way. But I still found it a desperately sad occasion. The tractors and trailers and 10-ton truck with the crates now moved up with hundreds of workers and the research team. Every elephant was properly measured, a host of scientific data collected, and then the contractors set about cutting up the carcasses.

The baby elephants, with a great deal of effort, were lifted and loaded into the crates on the back of the truck and returned to base camp at Ngweshla. As soon as we had loaded them into our own crates, we set off on the 265-mile return trip to Chipangali.

Mukwa was 46 inches high at the shoulder and Muchibi 48 inches. Both have thrived at the orphanage and are great favorites with the public, particularly the children. And both turned out to be "stars" in the TV series "Orphans of the Wild."

CHAPTER TWENTY

OSTRICHES, SNAKES & MORE

AS A NEWLY HATCHED ostrich chick, Ben stood 14 inches tall when his head was raised high. His back was covered with coarse, black and white bristles, and he looked much like a hedgehog, especially when he lay flat in the grass to escape detection. He had a creamy-white velvety down on his belly while his neck was soft and covered with fawn down, dappled with black spots. He had beautiful yellow eyes and stout legs with only two toes. The big toe supported a very large strong nail, which would become a dangerous weapon when he reached adulthood.

When Ben was a year old he stood 3 feet 6 inches tall and had developed large brown feathers and white wing-tips. His owner, a woman who lived near Bulawayo, had reared him from birth. As he matured he developed a taste for pegs from her clothesline, and thought nothing of eating them. Those he did not swallow he broke into pieces. She decided it was time he moved to Chipangali.

Moving a 200-pound ostrich is not easy. First, catch your ostrich. As soon as anyone went near him he kicked out with his powerful legs and we all scattered. We tried throwing a blanket over his head but he flicked if off and charged us without hesitation. Eventually we got a couple of long ropes and managed to trip him, whereupon six Africans pounced on him as he hit the ground. He never stopped kicking and fighting, and only after a long struggle were his legs tied together. From then on it was easy. It was only a seven-mile trip to Chipangali, but even in that short distance Ben nearly died. Ostriches are difficult birds to transport and can easily die of stress. Also, if held down they often damage their legs.

By the time we reached Chipangali, Ben was lying with his mouth open, panting heavily, and his long neck lay limp against the side of the vehicle. It was a hot day so we sprayed water over him and massaged his legs. He quickly recovered and joined two other ostriches at the orphanage, soon behaving as though he owned the place. Before long he became the "boss" of the large paddock in which he lived. He taught the other ostriches all of his bad habits, and before long they would attack anyone entering their territory.

Our young assistant, Terry, had to go into the paddock one day to check a baby duiker. Suddenly Ben attacked him. I had warned Terry not to go into the enclosure without a large stick. Ben kicked him severely many times and when help arrived he was badly bruised and bleeding, and in a state of shock. Ben was driven off and Terry rescued, feeling very sorry for himself.

On several occasions ostriches had chased one or another of the Chipangali workers, and the scene was always hilarious as one of the large birds sprinted after someone through thorn trees and long grass. But it was not always one-sided. One day I noticed Ben running flat out across his large enclosure, taking great strides as he bounced along. Chasing him, at a tremendous pace, was a male guinea-fowl. I could hardly believe my eyes when I saw how afraid the great ostrich was of the diminutive game bird. If the ostrich stopped, the guinea would fly onto his back and peck his neck, setting the ostrich off again, with the guinea-fowl in hot pursuit.

At first I thought it all very funny, but after a while I realized this was no laughing matter. Several times the guinea drove Ben into the wire fence; he was obviously under terrible stress and almost exhausted. Eventually he collapsed into a corner of his paddock. The guinea flew onto his back again to deliver the *coup de grâce*. I rushed into the pen and drove the guinea-fowl off. Ben staggered to his feet as I approached, and managed to walk a short distance, wobbling as he moved. I was worried about him and stood guard until he recovered.

After the general disturbance, with antelope, ostriches, zebra and warthogs running in all directions, I hoped that the vendetta was over and the guinea had made peace. How wrong I was. As soon as I left, the guinea returned and Ben took off again into the long grass and acacia trees, with the tough little bird chasing him as fast as his short legs would take him.

I called my assistants and we tried to catch the guinea, but he ran much faster than us. And he could fly, and we could not. An hour later the relentless guinea-fowl was after Ben again and I could see that if this continued the ostrich would die of exhaustion. One of the two had to be removed from the paddock. We had nowhere else to put Ben, so the guinea had to go. But how to catch him. Four hours later we were still no further ahead, so I was forced to shoot the bird with my 12-gauge shotgun. It took a long time to revive Ben. While he was unable to move, Terry said, "Now that he's down, I'd like to give him a good kick in the backside."

Late every afternoon a flock of about 15 wild guinea-fowl flew into the paddock to feed on grain and foods thrown in for the animals. When they had enough they took off toward the Matopo Hills, where they roosted in some large fig trees. Next afternoon they would be back again, often at the same time the wild ducks flew in.

White-faced duck, red-billed teal and knob-billed duck ("knobbies") often dropped in at Chipangali for a free meal, but these were seasonal visits. They arrived shortly before the onset of the rains. Sometimes as many as 20 knobbies would visit our tame ducks and other waterfowl, and after a great deal of squabbling, feeding and fluttering, off they would go. It was a delight to hear a flock of ducks flying overhead, circling and whistling over the ponds many times before splashing down among the residents.

———————

A young man arrived one day with a pitch-black, red-knobbed coot. It had swallowed a fishhook; an 18-inch length of nylon line was hanging out of its mouth. Its rescuer had been sitting at a dam watching ducks and other birds, when he noticed this one trying to regurgitate something. To add to its problems, one foot was tangled in nylon line.

We tried all ways of getting the hook out of the duck's throat but it had penetrated the neck muscle. I had no alternative but to push the sharp point right through the skin. The whole barb and curved part was then cut off with a pair of pliers, and the rest of the hook and nylon cord were easily pulled out through the mouth. I treated the small wound and the bird seemed none the worse after its near-tragic experience.

The coot joined our collection and we watched it carefully for a couple of weeks. As soon as I was sure it could survive on its own again, it was set free at the dam where it was found and it swam off to join the other coots in the reeds.

———————

Flamingos are elegant and beautiful water birds. That strangely shaped beak has evolved so that it can filter microorganisms out of the highly saline waters in which it feeds. I had never thought of keeping one in captivity and no desire to see one in a cage, but running Chipangali is full of surprises!

A police Land-Rover pulled up at the museum one morning when I was still working there, and two officers carefully brought out a rather mutilated flamingo. It was a female, pure white and obviously immature. It had a broken wing, and its leg was fractured. The police said the bird had flown into a power line near Bulawayo and they had been asked to collect it and deliver it to me. My first thoughts were: "Broken leg — broken wing — special diet — I cannot see it surviving. Best to put it down." But it was so lovely and cocky, it seemed a pity to destroy it without trying.

"Oh, I'll try to fix it," I said to the policemen, "but with its special diet and being in such a mess, I would hate to promise anything."

"I'm sure you'll do your best," said one of them, and they left me holding the flamingo.

Back at Chipangali, we set the leg in plaster of Paris, and the wing — fortunately not as badly injured as I had thought — was also treated. Our long-legged white lady was all set for a six-week immobile existence.

Paddy had an ingenious inspiration: she would use a long piece of mutton cloth as a hammock. Two holes were cut in it for the legs to dangle through, and the hammock was slung in a small cage. At first the bird refused to stick its beak into the messy special diet we prepared, but we persisted and two days later it was taking it with great relish.

The bird throve on its artificial diet and from time to time we would remove it from its hammock-sling to exercise its legs and wings. It became very tame and not only survived but did well in its new environment. Eventually we removed its bandages and set it free in a large aviary. It was touching to see the lovely bird take its first bath for many weeks in a large pond in the aviary. Paddy and I felt very proud of our achievements with such a difficult patient, and almost wept with delight at having saved the bird.

Although Margo, as she was named, will never be able to return to the wilds, she is perfectly happy in the big aviary with plenty of food, a pond, several ducks and other waterbirds as company — and no power lines to threaten her!

––––––––––

Another great bird with long slender legs is the crested crane. In addition to its superb color, it sports a most unusual top-notch. Crested cranes are royal game in Zimbabwe and we never attempted to collect them. One day, however, a farmer's wife arrived at Chipangali with two. One, "Herbie," she had had as a pet for some years. It was allowed to roam freely and often flew long distances and would stay away for days at a time. It was hit by a car one day and one wing was badly broken. A veterinary surgeon placed a metal pin in the wing, which healed perfectly, but since the bird could never fly again, it was brought to Chipangali.

The second bird had been brought to the farm as a tiny baby, and the farmer's wife had started rearing it. Rather than try to keep it, she decided it should keep Herbie company at Chipangali. The young bird, also a male, did well on a diet of

Margo the flamingo

grain, bread and occasional pieces of meat, and eventually took off and flew to a nearby dam. He often returned and would stay a few days before going off again. Each time his excursions became longer and finally he disappeared altogether. We like to think that he joined up with others of his own species in the wild and found a mate.

Herbie was not so lucky and will have to spend the rest of his days at Chipangali with duiker, impala, and other animals and birds as company. He has a habit of pecking visitors when he can get close enough, so he is not popular. Paddy refused to go into the wildfowl area unless Herbie was removed, for he had given her several nasty pecks on her legs, and one day Kevin got a deep wound from him. I was afraid that he might peck a small child, so I moved him to a large pen near our duiker and impala.

One of my favorite birds is the secretary bird. Its crest resembles an old-fashioned quill pen — hence the name secretary bird. We have had several over the years and each one arrived with a broken wing. They have tremendous stamina and heal quickly, and in no time take off again. Soon after moving to Chipangali, on two separate occasions secretary birds with injured wings were brought to us for attention.

What amazes me is their ability to hop. Even with a wing in plaster a secretary bird is able to hop over a six-foot fence, as our injured ones often proved. They start dancing about with the good wing spread out, and after a series of long hops and half flaps would leap the fence and disappear into the long grass. Once out, they would run like a wild-dog and the chase was on. Everyone available would sprint after the bird as it leapt, hopped, bounced and half-flew over rocks and small bushes. Up to two hours would be wasted trying to catch them. When their wings healed and they took off for good, I was delighted to see the last of them.

One day we received an adult spotted eagle owl from a lady in Bulawayo who had cared for it for several months. We placed it in a cage with eight young barn owls we were rearing, and the spotted eagle owl at once took a maternal interest in the chicks.

That very evening a large dish of chopped meat was brought for the babies and I was about to feed each owl separately with a chunk of meat. Suddenly the eagle owl hopped to the door of the cage, grabbed a piece of meat, returned to where the babies were sitting and fed it to one of them. She returned to the dish and repeated the procedure. I was surprised by her action, but placed the dish of meat closer to the babies and watched. She fed each baby until they had all had enough, then she had a good meal herself.

Next evening I merely placed the dish of meat near her and she again kindly fed all the babies. A few days later four more baby barn owls were brought in by the

Four young ostriches at Chipangali Wildlife Orphanage

It's feeding time at Chipangali

police. They were put into the cage with the existing eight. To my great delight, "Spottie" fed and looked after all 12 chicks, saving me a job. As the babies matured, they were released to fend for themselves, and Spottie's task became less and less, until she alone remained at Chipangali. She has a damaged wing and will never fly again. She has been with us for more than three years and now has eight other once-injured spotted eagle owls for company.

Our friend Tawny, is a tawny eagle reared successfully in Zimbabwe by a well-known conservationist. When he was about a year old he was set free. A split-ring with a number had been placed on his leg so that if found at a later date he could be traced to his owner. Two days after his release he was found over 70 miles away, almost dead from hunger and exhaustion. He was brought to Chipangali and now lives a life of ease in a large aviary which he shares with a ground hornbill, a bateleur eagle, several Wahlberg's eagles, a few kites and a number of crows.

Had Tawny not been rescued, it would have been assumed that he had successfully adapted to the wild. He loves people, and most visitors to Chipangali admire him. He has character and personality, and when spoken to will call with delight and fly to the side of his cage. Lovely as he is, he can be dangerous. One day a TV man went into his cage, and Tawny attacked him, clawing his arm and drawing blood. The man then had to rush out of the cage as Tawny was ready to have another go. Judging by the noise he made, he was serious about discouraging strangers in his territory.

Tawny has done the same to me. One evening at feeding time, with about 50 visitors watching, I entered the cage with a dish of meat. Tawny flew over my head, and without warning grabbed me on the head with both sets of claws, sinking them into my scalp. Blood flowed freely from eight deep cuts, and trickled down my face and neck and onto my shirt. I looked a real mess.

Most embarrassed, I slipped off to the house to clean my wounds and change my clothes. In spite of his cheekiness, Tawny is still one of my favorites at the orphanage and I admire his pluck and courage. He and the leopard, Ingwe, are very much alike. Both magnificent, both cheeky and dangerous, yet both most attractive and lovable.

Since a very early age, I don't think I have ever been without pet reptiles. Long before I knew anything about mammals and birds I studied snakes, and at one time I planned to start a snake park of my own in Natal, and then again in Zambia. Eventually it materialized in Zimbabwe.

208

A spotted eagle owl found injured on the main road near Bulawayo

Batalour eagle — one of the many eagles at Chipangali

When Chipangali Wildlife Orphanage started, it became obvious that many visitors wanted to see snakes and crocodiles even though they were not orphaned, ex-pets or sick. I realized that a collection of reptiles would be an additional attraction and could help support the orphanage.

We built several snake and lizard pits and also a large log cabin in which 10 glass cases were installed to house the smaller species. But snakes were not easy to come by. Most people are afraid to capture them, so the collection expanded slowly. Puff adders and Egyptian cobras are common species in Matabeleland and many were brought to us from Bulawayo where they were caught in suburban gardens.

While in eastern Zambia I studied the snakes and tortoises of the region. The work on tortoises involved incubation periods, distribution and growth, and as a final project I worked on the reptiles and amphibians of the Nyika Plateau in Malawi and Zambia. I continued my research into reptile reproduction when I arrived in Rhodesia and over the years hatched many species of snakes from eggs collected.

To my great delight a native arrived at Chipangali one day in 1973 with a clutch of 25 python eggs, found in an unused mine shaft. There was no sign of the mother so he brought the eggs to me for identification. I recognized them immediately and opened two to see what stage of incubation they had reached. Both appeared very fresh and newly laid, but obviously I could not say exactly how many days old.

The remaining 23 eggs were placed in a wooden box with leaf-litter and sand, and kept warm and damp at all times. Three months after they had been brought in, I opened the box to sprinkle some warm water over them, and to my surprise saw it was alive with young pythons. I counted them as I removed them and found that 15 of the eggs had hatched, and others showed signs of hatching. The remaining eggs were left, and next morning another four snakes were crawling about.

The rest of the batch was obviously bad and these were discarded. The incubation period was at least 98 days.

I released nine of the babies into the Matopo Hills and kept 10 for study purposes. Three died within a week, and two escaped, leaving me with only five. They were delightful creatures and my sons spent hours finding wild mice for them. They averaged about 18 inches long but varied in size quite a lot.

We kept the five pythons in a large outdoor enclosure with many other snakes. Unfortunately one died when a puff adder bit it, and another was eaten by a large Egyptian cobra. The remaining three were moved to an open enclosure with a large pond, trees and much grass, and are now thriving in near-natural conditions. As companions they have many tortoises, a few terrapins and a number of large grass snakes.

210

Viv demonstrates puff adder "milking" to a group of visitors

Kevin (left) and Barry help the author with an injured spotted eagle owl

Puff adders breed well in captivity and females produce their living young usually during the rains, from about November to March; each year we have numerous young ones to release back into the wild. Some of our females have produced as many as 45 young at a time but many die soon after birth, and wild crows take a fair number.

It is surprising how many snakes and young tortoises are stolen from Chipangali. One has to watch the young male visitors very carefully in the snake area. They think nothing of leaping over the wall and helping themselves to a little tortoise, a terrapin, or even brown house snakes and other non-poisonous varieties.

But no one will pinch Winnie the crocodile. He weighs just over 480 pounds, and is more than 12 feet long, one of the finest crocodiles I have ever seen. His teeth are beautiful and white, very sharp, and all still in good shape despite his being at least 60 years old. Winnie was brought to Chipangali toward the end of 1976. The great reptile had been living on goats and donkeys in the communal lands along the Sabi River in eastern Zimbabwe. It was snared with a "noose-trap," drugged and brought to Chipangali.

It is amazing how many phone calls I receive during the summer asking me to collect or identify snakes. On hundreds of occasions people have asked me to remove a snake from their garden or house.

A miner drove nearly 60 miles to Chipangali to fetch me one day to help him get rid of a very large snake which had taken up residence in a shaft at his little gold mine. He had a gang of miners working on a long prospecting tunnel into the side of the hill where he was looking for a gold reef. One morning his workers went into the shaft for the day's work and were suddenly confronted with this large reptile. They came screaming out of the tunnel and refused to go in again until the mine manager removed it. The manager was no hero either and refused to go into the mine. He decided I was the answer to his problem.

Armed with a powerful torch and long stick, I moved very slowly into the mine flashing the light from side to side of the tunnel as I went, not knowing what kind of snake was there. It might have been a large black mamba, a cobra or even a large python. The miner had merely said it was a large snake — and that could mean anything.

At the very end of the tunnel, my torch light caught the beautiful glossy coils of an enormous python. It lay coiled in a slight depression and made no effort to move as I approached it. It was difficult to tell how long it was but I judged it to be at least 10 feet.

It was cold in the mine and the snake was most lethargic. I had no difficulty grabbing it by the head, after first pinning it down with my stick. It struggled and threw a couple of coils around my arms but once I had it by the head, with one hand, and the tail with the other hand, it was easy enough to manage.

It weighed at least 85 pounds, and after capturing it, I realized it was much longer than my first guess of 10 feet. As I came out of the mine with the great reptile, there was a sudden scattering of workers and none of them would touch it at first. A few minutes later, however, I persuaded one of the miners to stroke it, and suddenly all the others became brave and wanted to touch the snake.

I put it into a large grain bag with the top securely tied with wire and took it back to Chipangali. Later I found a most suitable place to release it — a site at the edge of the Matopo Hills close to the national park, where it was safe and would not be molested by man. It was also a long way from the mine, and since I did not get another call from them, presumably the snake did not return.

We measured the python before releasing it, and it was more than 15 feet long, a truly magnificent reptile, and I am delighted that the miners did not kill it when it was first seen. Too often that is the first instinctive action when people see a snake — even the most harmless of them.

CHAPTER TWENTY-ONE

DUIKERS OF AFRICA

DUIKERS, THE MOST primitive of all African antelope, are also the "brainiest," having the biggest brains in relation to body size. They vary in size from the beautiful, tiny (16 inches high at the shoulder) blue duiker to their yellow-backed cousins which are more than twice the size.

The duiker (meaning "diver") gets its name from its habit of diving into thick bush or undergrowth with incredible speed, its head held low and back arched.

There are two classes of duiker — those which live in open savannah country and those found in thick bush and forests. They are found in Africa from sea level right up to 14,000 feet — on the slopes of Mount Kenya.

Very little is known about their behavior. Some species are active in the day, such as the little blue duiker which is often seen in the early morning or the late afternoon. If they feel threatened they will "freeze" where they stand or, if they have time they'll move into a thicket, camouflaging themselves behind a tree or fallen stump. A baby duiker will often lie down and remain as still as a statue, immobile even if an intruder comes right up beside it.

The blue duiker has been poached almost to the point of extinction in Zimbabwe. I once found more that 200 of the cruel wire snares which are set for these animals, imposing an agonizing, lingering death for the victims.

There is hardly an indigenous forest in Africa without some of its species in it. They are the most dominant forest antelope, and although they are particularly partial to shady areas, they are adaptable and the common duiker can survive in relatively dry habitat.

Because they are so shy and secretive, and in many cases live in almost impenetrable areas, there is still a great deal to learn about the duiker. In fact, there is still much confusion over their classification. But in spite of their elusiveness, in many parts of the continent they are now in danger of extinction. One of the reasons is the wholesale devastation of Africa's forests.

About 100 acres of tropical rain forest are disrupted every minute of every day. The FAO (Food and Agricultural Organization) estimated that Uganda has lost more than two-thirds of its forest cover. The fate of the tropical rain forests will be, in my opinion, one of the major factors affecting the quality of life in Africa and eventually, the fate of its inhabitants. If the forests are destroyed, soil erosion will follow, then desertification, and life will be very hard for the people.

Dr. Kenton Miller wrote in 1986 that 277,000 acres of tropical forests are felled and burned every year, and at that rate they will all disappear by the year 2071.

"The most valuable and the richest in species, the lowland rain forests, are unlikely to survive to the end of the century," he wrote.

"If the forests are to be saved they must be economically viable and socially acceptable at national and local levels. The flora and fauna will only be truly secure when the people who make a living from the tropical forests can produce more food and goods than they themselves need."

Those areas where people pose no threat to ecosystem stability should be protected to allow the floral and faunal products to be harvested. The numbers of duiker in the wild in Africa are going down, in some cases drastically. Jentink's duiker, found in Liberia and the Ivory Coast, is on the point of extinction. Certain species in Tanzania, Kenya, Sierra Leone, Zimbabwe and Rwanda are now very rare, because of poaching, hunting and the vanishing forests. Twelve African countries provide the habitat of about 15 species, or 95 percent of all the continent's duikers.

The importance of saving the forests cannot be overstressed. They provide the foundation for the human, animal and vegetable life which they support. Remove them and the rest will deteriorate and collapse. The forests could be saved and renewed but today are being devastatingly abused and mismanaged. Some forest areas, like the Sapo National Park in Liberia and the Tai Forest in neighboring Ivory Coast need urgent and special protection.

There will have to be international and regional cooperation to bring Africa out of this crisis, but it is basically each individual country's responsibility to examine its resources and set acceptable targets for balanced conservation and management, and proper use of the tropical forests. What happens to the tropical forests is sometimes

Small carnivore pens at Chipangali

Part of the Chipangali Tea Gardens

a symptom of what can go wrong when well-intentioned foreign aid does not take into account long-term ecological factors.

Dr. Kenton Miller made a valid point when he wrote in 1986: "It is one thing to sit in comfort and argue that everyone's survival depends on keeping tropical forests intact, but this kind of ideology cannot be expected to mean much to the average farm, road, or sawmill laborer in the tropics, whose survival may depend on deforestation."

The indigenous people living in and close to the forest, and depending on it, the small farmers, the foresters, and all those who use it daily in one way or another, must take part in the management and planning projects if they are to have any hope of success.

Sound statistics and meticulously accurate information are essential if development agencies' plans to conserve tropical forest environments are to succeed. Planning without foreknowledge is a recipe for ecological disaster.

The Special Survival Commission of the International Union for Conservation of Nature and Natural Resources (of which I am a member) recently set up the Antelope Specialist Group which is sponsoring the 10-year survey of the duikers of Africa. This is recognition of the vital importance of the problems just discussed.

This duiker survey is particularly important because its subject's habitat is generally the rain forest. As I cannot say too often, the preservation of the rain forest is critical to the whole ecological future of the continent.

The Survey Team intends to visit Ghana, the Ivory Coast, Liberia, Sierra Leone and Guinea in West Africa; Kenya, Tanzania, Uganda, Rwanda and Burundi in East Africa; the Central African Republic, Cameroon, Gabon and the Congo; and in Southern Africa, South Africa and Namibia. It may be necessary to mount more than one expedition to each area. Surveys will also be carried out in Ethiopia, Malawi, Botswana, Zaire, Zambia, Senegal, Gambia and Niger.

Chipangali will be playing an important part in the survey. The cells making up the living parts of a duiker's body will be studied under microscopes. Skulls, skin and teeth will be measured, analyzed and recorded, and a master map of Africa will show exactly where each specimen was collected. Zoos will be visited, people who keep live duiker as pets will be asked to cooperate. At the Chipangali Orphanage in Bulawayo, careful study of the mating habits and gestation periods will be made much more easily than could possibly be done in the wild.

We began our field work in January 1986 and it is expected to take the full 10 years to cover the main study areas. One major expedition a year will be undertaken,

218

lasting from one to six months. Each year a different region will be visited and an essential duty will be the collection of duiker specimens.

For the survey to succeed we will have to secure the willing cooperation of all the African governments concerned. Since we represent a widely respected scientific organization, this we expect to get. In the end we hope to present a well-documented register of the duiker of Africa, showing where they live, and how they live; their predators; their habitat; and the diseases they get. A valuable by-product of the project should be clarification of the somewhat confused list of subspecies of duiker.

Underpinning the whole study will be the distribution and condition of the evergreen forests, the duiker's principal habitat, and this will help contemporary and future ecologists to seek a way to save the forests, and consequently the continent, from devastation. We are making a contribution to posterity.

CHAPTER TWENTY-TWO

CHIPANGALI ON TV

W HAT A SAD WORLD it would be if everybody's attitude toward the sick and the maimed, the young, the helpless, the lost, was: "Let them fend for themselves; nature must take its course."

We care for our fellow humans; we look after our injured dogs and cats and cure and save them when we can. Why should it be different with other creatures which will die if not helped? There are those who prefer to turn their backs on injured wild animals. We at Chipangali take an opposite view. There is a great deal of satisfaction in the work we do, and the measure of support from hundreds of people who share our conscience in this respect has made Chipangali a most rewarding experience.

The inhabitants of the western world's ever-growing cities have moved further and further away from nature and wild animal life. In most of southern Africa, and particularly Zimbabwe, the bush, the animals and the birds are still close to all but the biggest cities. Not surprisingly hundreds of young animals have become pets for one reason or another. There is hardly a wild animal, or bird, or for that matter even a reptile, that someone will not want to take home, possibly without the faintest idea how to care for it.

The most common pets in Zimbabwe are vervet monkeys and baboons. Hedgehogs and night apes are often kept, as well as mongooses, duiker, steenbok and jackals. Some people have acquired "tame" warthogs, bush pigs and even young kudu. On farms and in rural areas, leopards, servals, hyena and giraffe can sometimes be found in gardens, but only until the animals become a nuisance.

I believe that to take a wild animal from its natural habitat is a loss to nature, not only of that animal, but of all the progeny that would have been born had it been left undisturbed. To me, it is vitally important that the animal be born, live naturally, produce young and die in its own community. It should not be kept in captivity in a house, remote from its natural environment.

Over the 35 years that I have worked in various fields of wildlife, I have looked after and reared almost every species of mammal found in Zimbabwe, from elephant to the smallest rodents and shrews. I have overwhelming evidence that most non-domesticated wild animals make unsuitable pets for a variety of reasons. Many harbor disease. City dwellers, people in high density areas, have to confine the animal to a kitchen, garage, or in the house. Because people do not know what the animal should eat, many are starved. They pine from loneliness when they lack a mate. They seldom get enough exercise. Often they become dangerous, and can pose a serious threat to children, and even adults. To keep animals happy and healthy, suitable cages, or runs, must be provided and few of their owners are prepared to spend the money. There is always the risk that the animal will escape and cause havoc in the neighborhood, hurt a child or elderly person, or itself be killed on the road, or by dogs or cats.

I have tried to release hundreds of hand-reared animals back into the wild. In most cases, though not all, the results have been disappointing. Few survive the harsher, competitive environment. It takes a great deal of time and patience to successfully return animals to the wild. When dealing with large numbers of orphaned animals, the task is many times more formidable.

I have noticed time and time again the emotional attachment of a young animal to the human who rears it. The baby forms a social relationship with its foster-parent. This is sometimes referred to as "imprinting." Most small antelope, raised on the bottle, become strongly attached to the person rearing it. It will have little to do with others of its same species. Most herd-animals are well developed at birth and the critical period of imprinting takes place within a few days of life. Antelope calves with this background are not afraid of dogs and as a result they are often killed by these marauding animals.

Wild animals are generally orphaned as a result of the mother being killed by a predator, killed by a car, or shot by a hunter. Often they are found cold and weak, sick, wounded or injured, and if left will certainly die. People take in an animal with the best of motives, usually feeling sorry for it, and this is quite understandable. Again, I would like to mention that the kindest thing, in the long run, is to leave the animal and let nature take its course.

Nine times out of ten the "sick, starving and deserted" animal has been hidden by its mother while she's away looking for food. Most antelope mothers, especially the duiker and steenbok, hide their young for several weeks before the baby is old enough to accompany her on daily feeding trips. The mother can be hiding very close by, and will come and feed the baby as soon as the intruder leaves.

On the other hand, not all wild animals that end up in captivity are "saved" by well-meaning humans. Many people go into the bush with the intention of trapping young animals for pets. Female wild animals with babies are often shot so that the hunter can capture the infant.

It is only when they are bitten, or when a child is bitten or scratched, or even when they are kept awake nights, that these pet owners look for another home for it. Some merely dump the animal they have so carefully looked after, others send them to a zoo, while some have the animal killed. But for every person who dumps a pet there are a dozen others who really do care.

I have seen hundreds of people at Chipangali weep openly when parting with a wild pet. They pay for its maintenance and write to us regularly to see how it is getting on. For them I have the greatest admiration. Most really did save the animal in the first place, and brought it to us to make sure that it would be safe and happy.

Chipangali Wildlife Orphanage is unique in central and southern Africa. No other institution takes care of orphaned, injured, sick or abandoned wild animals. The orphanage is not a zoo nor a menagerie. We have not collected the animals for financial gain. Those creatures that can be released back into the wild go back. But for many, as I have explained, the traumatic experience of close association with humans, and the unnatural life in their formative months and years, makes that impossible. They will stay with us.

From time to time I have had doubts about whether we were doing the right thing. Now, the knowledge that we are helping to save the lives of many of the beautiful and often rare wild animals in this part of Africa, and have provided a unique opportunity for research, has convinced me that we were right. We place great emphasis at Chipangali on the educational value of the animals, birds and reptiles there.

I believe that if we are to save the wildlife of Africa we must get the message through to the children. Hence our emphasis on the value of education. Hundreds of classes of schoolchildren of all ages have visited the orphanage since its inception. Lectures are given on all aspects of conservation. I have an all-round knowledge on all aspects of nature, be it herpetology, ornithology, mammalogy or even botany, and feel I can get the right message across.

School classes that are involved in a specific natural history project often use Chipangali. Many of the animals have been studied in detail by scholars. Biology students from the Teachers College are frequent visitors. It is time nature lovers realize that each year more and more species of wildlife are in danger of becoming extinct. Wildlife is not only for our aesthetic enjoyment but it is also of scientific value. The more our natural heritage is understood and appreciated, the greater are its chances of survival.

Chipangali stimulates a great interest in wildlife. The sight of a living animal has a far greater impact than one mounted in a museum, or pictured in a book. It is an irony of twentieth century Africa that today many of the urbanized black children, whose grandparents certainly, and probably even their parents, grew up among herds of antelope in the wild, know no more about the animal life of Africa than, say, a teen-ager in the Bronx in New York.

One of the most heart-warming experiences at Chipangali is to see a class of black schoolchildren absolutely fascinated at the sight of a troop of baboons, or watch the surprise on their faces when they see Sandy the lioness. Usually they can hardly believe that they are real and questions about the animals come thick and fast.

———

When Zimbabwe became independent in 1980, contrary to the fears of some people, instead of bringing new problems it meant just the opposite for our orphanage.

Zimbabwe's Minister of Natural Resources and Tourism, the Honorable Mrs. Victoria Chitepo, has been a staunch supporter of our work. She has made it clear that she will never let Chipangali close through lack of funds and support. In fact, we have had massive support for Chipangali since independence and our minister has proved to be the finest Minister of Natural Resources that this country has seen in the past 25 years. She has a genuine interest in wildlife and conservation, and has been a fearless, outspoken champion of conservation.

She has visited the orphanage on many occasions and it is always a great pleasure to welcome her.

Research in the breeding of endangered species in captivity is long overdue. Many zoos have made a start but much more work needs to be done. Conservation of endangered species is inseparable from scientific research, and if the species is already rare in the wild, the studies must be conducted with captive animals. The knowledge provided can then be used when dealing with the wild population. The success of breeding many species in captivity is only achieved with ideal conditions, and these can vary greatly from one species to the next. Considering that most of our animals at Chipangali are ex-pets, we are proud of the breeding results we have achieved.

224

Nowhere in southern or central Africa, or for that matter anywhere in Africa, has a place been set aside specifically for carnivore research. As a direct result of the activities of man, many of the world's carnivores, and especially the cats, have declined drastically over the last 30 years, and some are now threatened with extinction.

The cheetah and the leopard are hunted prodigiously, for their skins fetch high prices in Europe and America. As long as women wear expensive fur coats, the handsome spotted cats will be in danger. The carnivores are essential in their wild environment where they kill the weaker individuals, allowing the fitter and stronger prey animals to survive. They help preserve the balance of nature.

I would like to see a feline breeding station established where rare species could be studied and bred, and progeny returned to the wild to repopulate selected areas. If they are to be reintroduced to the wild they must be bred in conditions as close as possible to their natural habitat. They will still have to be taught to hunt, and large enclosures would be necessary for that.

An exciting new project with which Chipangali hopes to be associated is the establishment of a Rhino Breeding Center — a rhino "depot" where newly captured animals are kept while they get used to captivity and prepared for movement to American and European zoos, other African countries, or to one of Zimbabwe's own national parks. It would also be used for research where reproductive and feeding studies, among others, could be carried out. It is envisaged that up to 20 or more rhinos could be kept, but most of these would be in the Matopos National Park. Not more than four rhino will be kept at the orphanage itself, and these will be used mainly for educational purposes.

It would probably astonish some of my early schoolmasters to know that I have had well over 50 scientific papers published in some of the world's most respected scientific journals. For my thesis on game and tsetse fly in eastern Zambia in 1971, I became a Member of the Institute of Biologists in London. The shelves of my office are lined with my books and papers, the result of a lifetime of research.

But recently I began to realize that these works were "preaching" to the already converted, for the most part. The rather elite world of scientists is only a small percentage of people interested in wildlife. Chipangali has given me a unique opportunity to reach a far greater public through radio and television.

Television in particular knows no boundaries — beyond the limits of the transmitter — and thousands of viewers have now seen Chipangali, and learned about it, far beyond the shores of Africa.

The first TV program on Chipangali was called "Armchair Safari." The series of 13 studio "chats" on conservation, snakes, spiders and a wide range of nature subjects was so popular locally that another 13 followed — this time on wildlife in Botswana and other neighboring countries. It was equally successful and became a regular feature. Many of the 16mm wildlife films I had made during my service in Zambia were used in some of these programs.

Many of Chipangali's animals were very tame and manageable and could be taken to the TV studio. The shows were all "live" and each week I took a different animal. The TV "stars" included lion cubs, leopards, servals, caracals, snakes, wild-dog puppies, eagles and all kinds of monkeys. The public loved to watch the animals being handled, particularly because each show was impromptu.

The real break came when Bill Revolta, a director of a Zimbabwe film production house in Harare, conceived the idea of producing a wildlife TV series based on my book *Orphans of the Wild*, with American actor Marshall Thompson presenting it. We would use all of our animals at Chipangali. I would work with and handle the animals and Marshall would talk to me about them. The series was based around Chipangali. Paddy, Kevin and Barry would also be featured in the programs. I worked out the sequences and after much preparation, shooting began.

Marshall Thompson, with a crew of sound and camera people, and production assistants, stayed at a Bulawayo hotel. We filmed for more than six months in 1983, mostly at Chipangali. However, we had to do a fair amount of work away from the orphanage and selected several private game ranches in Zimbabwe where the filming could take place.

Many of the factual stories about the animals from *Orphans of the Wild* were re-enacted. It worked very well. It gave viewers some idea of what our orphanage was all about and how we had acquired some of our animals. Every day of filming brought new and interesting events, new problems and new adventures. We could never predict what would happen. Sometimes schedules would be upset because animals would become sick. So for the six months that the film crew was at Chipangali, many incidents were filmed spontaneously. We might be busy filming a chameleon eating a grasshopper when, unexpectedly, an African would arrive with a baby steenbok, a pangolin (anteater) or some other animal. Such incidents were filmed, unrehearsed, as they happened. These include the birth of a klipspringer, the arrival of a small antbear, the hatching of spotted eagles' eggs, etc.

We also had our own set program of returning animals to the wild and that went on, whether the television crew was there or not. Of course if we had an animal or group to be set free, we sometimes waited so that the sequence could be properly filmed. We never staged events such as returning animals to the wild for the sake of the TV series. They were all authentic. The release of jackals, porcupines and

Filming of TV series "Orphans of the Wild"

The author and his staff attending to an injured steenbok

genets to the wild, were planned prior to the TV series being organized.

We used a lot of footage from my own film library of events that had happened at Chipangali earlier. One of the most interesting was the return of a troop of vervet monkeys to the wild on an island in Lake Kariba. This had been filmed years before we knew a TV series was to be made.

We were always on the lookout for unusual or exciting incidents. Wildlife in Africa is full of surprises with or without television, so we found plenty in six months.

While we were in the wild I enjoyed the experiences, and got on well with the film directors and crew. It was all natural, and there was no time to lose. Everything was done quickly and efficiently. But at Chipangali it was another story . . .

My family and I would be up very early in the morning to organize the day's normal work of feeding baby animals, cleaning cages and enclosures, treating sick and injured animals, and a wide range of chores. We started before 6:00 A.M. The film crew would arrive at their leisure from 8:30 to 9:30, and start sorting cameras, films, tape recorders and other equipment. We would be lucky to begin shooting by 10:00 A.M.

I would place the animal to be filmed where it was required, with the correct light, and we would start. On the word "Action" Marshall and I began to talk about the animal, and after about 20 seconds we would hear "Cut." The camera had run out of film, or the tape recorder was not working, or there was a gremlin in the gate of the camera, or something else was wrong. We would hang about waiting while the problem was sorted out, and once more "Action" would be called.

By this time, the serval, or caracal or leopard which I was trying to hold had had enough of it all (and so would I) and the "star" would either bite me, or run off the set. "Cut" they would yell, and once again we would try to get everything and everyone in place. By this time I would be chasing the animal to be filmed, getting thoroughly dirty in the process. Once again "Action" would be called. This time the production assistant or someone would notice my fingernails were dirty. "Cut" they would call. I'd clean my nails and five minutes later we would start again.

I have wonderful patience with animals or any form of wildlife, but when it comes to cameramen and recording people, I am afraid I just do not have it in similar measure. After hours of doing some of the sequences, up to as many as 13 times, it was just too much and I told everyone so in no uncertain terms. What I found especially demanding was the "one more 'take' for luck" when the first "take" was usually a good one, and we were then already on the 10th!

After several hours of filming, I was not a pleasant person to work with, as I'm sure those who were there will verify. By the end of the day the film crew and

Marshall would go back to their hotel, have a good hot bath and spend the rest of the evening leisurely enjoying drinks and dinner. My family and I would be getting on with the very demanding business of running the day-to-day affairs of Chipangali.

Next day we would start all over again. But I'll be the first to admit that in the end it was all worthwhile.

CHAPTER TWENTY-THREE

WE HAVE WON!

NINETY-NINE out of 100 visitors to Chipangali give us pleasure in their interest and the way they behave. But the wicked one percent are more of a nuisance than our most mischievous animals.

One afternoon I caught two young men giving gin to the baboons, feeding it to them in a lemonade bottle. Once a woman visitor, not long out from England, leaned into the snake pit and deliberately poked the spike of her umbrella through the head of my largest female puff adder. It seems that many newcomers to Africa from Britain and Europe are irresponsible and stupid, probably through ignorance of the potential dangers.

I have seen mothers watch benignly as their children chase each other on the walls of the snake pit where one slip would land them among the deadly puff adders and cobras below. Others allow their children to climb over protective barriers to feed the animals or poke their fingers into the cages. They say, "It serves him right if he is bitten, and then he'll learn!" But when it actually happens it's quite a different story.

The Africans are the best behaved visitors. Their children are always quiet and never tease the animals or climb over the barrier fences.

Some of the questions we get have the same theme. At the cheetah's cage it is usually: "Why is he so savage, growling like that all the time?" and I have to explain: "He's actually purring with contentment, like a cat with a saucer of milk. Would you like to go into the cage and stroke him?"

Proximity with a caged animal seems to bring out the worst in some people, like putting them behind the wheel of an automobile, and it is by no means always children who behave like this.

A grown man, kicking at the caracal's cage, asks smugly: "Oh, Mr. Wilson, why is this animal so vicious?" and I have to leave out the words "You idiot" when I reply: "Because you are kicking the wire and teasing him."

By far the majority of visitors are sympathetic and understanding. Many Bulawayo residents find pleasure in a trip to Chipangali and return time and again with friends and relatives from elsewhere. Were it not for their kindness and generosity we would not have survived and the orphanage would have closed long ago.

Help has come to Chipangali in many ways, but the "adoption plan" was our greatest benefactor. It all started with a friend who was studying servals. When I was at the museum he was a frequent caller, gathering information for his research project. Later he came to Chipangali, and when he learned we were having financial difficulty, said: "Viv, how much would it cost to feed the servals?" I said, off the cuff, "About $15 a month for the pair." "OK," he said, "I will adopt them and pay for their food." He went on: "They must naturally stay at Chipangali, and I will give you a $15 check each month." We had never heard of anything like this before — but it sounded like a great idea and we were delighted.

We made a little sign and stuck it on the serval cage: "These servals have been adopted by Les and Jean Cross of Bulawayo." Soon more animals were adopted as news of the plan spread, and before long at least half of our orphans had foster parents. This financial help enabled us to keep going.

Another inspiration was the formation of the Friends of Chipangali Society. Orphanage enthusiasts soon had thriving branches in Bulawayo and Harare, and as a result of donations we could buy a beautiful cage for Ingwe the leopard and make improvements throughout, including new equipment in the animal hospital.

Things seemed to be going very well, but it did not last. In 1980 Zimbabwe attained its independence and Mrs. Victoria Chitepo was appointed Minister of Natural Resources. The social structure of the country was changing and many of our supporters left. However, we found in Minister Chitepo a new ally.

The Friends of Chipangali Society was changed in 1980 to the Chipangali Wildlife Trust under the chairmanship of Sir Athol Evans (who has written the Foreword to this book).

By 1984, the Chipangali project had become too big for one person to finance and manage. The Trust took over the orphanage in April, and I was appointed to manage it as Director. A massive fund raising campaign was launched to finance the operation. Paddy and I were to hand over the animals, buildings, vehicles and fixed assets as a gift to the Trust.

The author with an orphaned leopard

Unfortunately only a few thousand dollars was raised. One sad day the Trustees told us they could not raise enough money and they would have to drop the project. Paddy, the boys and I were back to "Square One" and would have to battle along on our own. Most of the Trustees resigned, but Sir Athol Evans and Dr. Jon Hulme continued their efforts to help save the orphanage.

Word soon got around that the end of Chipangali was near. Suddenly, miraculously it seemed, things began to change. Sheila Whyte, a newspaper reporter, wrote a series of articles on the orphanage, creating a lot of interest, and funds began to pour in. The Trust was reconstituted, new Trustees were appointed and everything improved.

The real break came when the TV series "Orphans of the Wild" was first shown in southern and central Africa. Things got better and better, and in April 1987, the Trust again took over the orphanage, this time for good.

My family and I gave all the animals to the Trust and we leased the land and buildings for a nominal sum of one dollar a year. I have remained in charge as Honorary Director and Kevin and Barry are responsible for the day-to-day running of the orphanage. Paddy is administrator of the organization. We have a splendid team.

I plan now to concentrate full time on my Duiker Survey of Africa. At long last we have the funds and time to devote to this massive research program — after years of battling with the odds often stacked against us.

Chipangali has succeeded. It has survived. We have won!

PHOTO CREDITS

*All color photos in this volume
were taken by Viv Wilson*